jewish cooking
jewish cooks

Ramona Koval

photography by Robert Reichenfeld

NEW HOLLAND

*For my daughters—Emma and Sara
and my granddaughters Maya, Eden and Bella*

contents

foreword

The paradox of Jewish 'cuisine' is that it doesn't exist. Not as a single, definable entity. Probably the closest one can come to a definition of Jewish food is that it is one religion, but many food styles. At its base is a set of food proscriptions: its one constant is its dietary laws.

With such a wide diaspora over five millennia, Jewish people adapted regionally and cooked the foods available in the areas in which they found themselves. Thus Jewish food has been the most adapted and interpreted in the world. The food of the ancient Hebrews bears little resemblance to what was eaten in Odessa or Minsk. Claudia Roden, author of the The Book of Jewish Food sees it as a kaleidoscope: 'Jewish food is about remembering and adapting. It is essentially nostalgic.' However Jewish food has two distinct branches, a north-south divide between Ashkenazi food of Eastern and Western Europe, and Sephardi food of the Mediterranean, the Middle East and North Africa. In northern Europe, goose fat, rendered chicken fat (schmaltz) and butter replaced the olive oil of ancient Egypt and the Mediterranean. 'When Ashkenazi Jews were confined to ghettoes,' Roden observes, 'a particular culture developed, and also a cuisine. Because they were confined, their culture and their gastronomy crystalised in a certain way. Those dishes then became part of a cuisine which they kept up as their own, and which defined their identity.' And then recipes were adapted yet again when they arrived in Australia.

Ramona Koval, one of Australia's most loved and respected broadcasters and columnists, has collected a smorgasbord of recipes in this utterly charming, frequently moving, volume. It is a personal social history of migration and adaptation, not just of Ramona's own family but of friends and their extended families. In Poland in 1942, Ramona's luckily-blond Jewish mother was packed off with false papers to live in Warsaw with a Gentile family. The last time she sat down at her own mother's table was when she was 13. Yet, in Melbourne in the 1950s, she set about re-creating—from taste—the scantly-remembered dishes of her childhood for her young family.

Crammed with anecdotes and personal reminiscences, the book is a collection of memories, tastes and smells. It is a celebration of the many (mainly Ashkenazi) cooking traditions that have arrived in Australia. It also shows how various dishes have been adapted even after they've migrated here. For instance the ABC's Dr Norman (Swirsky) Swan makes changes to his Glasgow mother's long-cooked Sabbath stew, cholent. (Much to his mother's disapproval, Swan unauthentically soaks his lima beans first to reduce their flatulent effect). Animal rights activist and philosopher Peter Singer adapts Viennese ponchkes to a non-dairy version, substituting soy milk. Using food as the key, this wonderful book unlocks the rich heritage of this disparate cultural group which has profoundly enriched Australian life.

Cherry Ripe

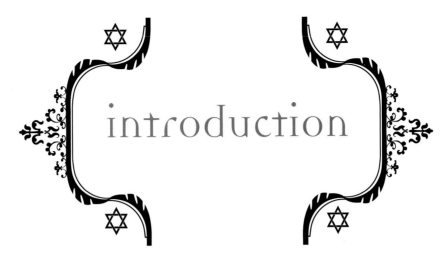

introduction

Iike all other traditional foods, Jewish food is imbued with many meanings, both ritual and emotional. Jews have created a great eating culture, unlike the Irish or the Germans, who are great drinkers. Jewish drunks are rare, but go down the list at an Eaters Anonymous meeting, and you may as well be looking at the guest list to a Passover feast. Jews might not understand why you need the right wine with dinner, or a beer at the end of the day, or a whisky nightcap, but they are aghast at the suggestion that just one kind of cake is enough for most people.

Food is important to Jews as a way of expressing our ritual traditions. Eating and drinking are thought of as religious acts, as are most other things in the day. When I was a child my mother seemed to know a prayer for everything—picking the first fruit from the tree, washing hands, seeing a falling star, or putting on a new dress.

'Kosher' means 'proper'—and the laws of 'Kashrus' define what is kosher. They govern what is to be eaten, how it is to be prepared, what it is to be combined with, how it is to be served and by whom. Implicit in the idea of kosher food is that every action is governed by religious laws, so that by following God's laws for each and every step, you are reminded that God is everywhere. The Torah scholar Philo of Alexandria (Philo Judaeus; 20 BC–40 AD) said that the dietary laws are supposed to teach us control over our bodily appetites and that Moses forbade us pork, which was the most delicious of all meats, to discourage excessive self-indulgence. A thousand years after Philo, Maimonides, an important Jewish theologian and philosopher, agreed, and added the view that all the forbidden foods are unwholesome or bad for the health.

Jewish dietary laws arise from a few passages in the Old Testament when God told Moses and his brother Aaron to tell the Jews:

These are the living things which ye may eat among all the beasts that are on the earth. Whatsoever parteth the hoof, and is wholly cloven footed, and cheweth the cud, among the beasts, that ye may eat. Nevertheless these shall ye not eat of them that only chew the cud, or of them that only part the hoof: the camel because he only cheweth the cud but parteth not the hoof, he is unclean to you. And the rock badger, because he cheweth the cud, but parteth not the hoof, he is unclean to you, and the hare because he cheweth the cud...and the swine because he parteth the hoof, and is cloven footed, but cheweth not the cud, he is unclean unto you. Of their flesh ye shall not eat, and their carcasses ye shall not touch; they are unclean unto you. These may ye eat of all that are in the waters; whatsoever hath fins and scales in the waters, in the seas and in the rivers, them may ye eat...and these ye shall have in detestation among the fowls; they shall not be eaten, they are a detestable thing: the eagle, the great vulture, and the bearded vulture, and the osprey: and the kite and the falcon after its kinds: every raven after its kinds: and the ostrich and the nighthawk, and the sea-mew and the hawk after its kinds: and the little owl and the cormorant and the great owl: and the horned owl and the pelican

and the carrion vulture: and the stork and the heron after its kinds, and the hoopoe and the bat. All winged swarming things that go upon all fours are a detestable thing unto you. Yet these may ye eat of all winged swarming things that go upon all fours, which have jointed legs above their feet, wherewith to leap upon the earth: even these of them ye may eat: the locust after its kinds, and the cricket after its kinds, and the grasshopper after its kinds…and these are they which are unclean unto you among the swarming things that swarm on the earth: and the weasel and the mouse, and the great lizard after its kinds, and the gecko, and the land-crocodile, and the lizard and the chameleon.
Leviticus 11:1–30

And ye shall eat no manner of blood, whether it be of fowl or of beast, in any of your dwellings. Whosoever it be that eateth any blood, that soul shall be cut off from his people.
Leviticus 7:26–27

Mama explained to me that it was considered immoral to cook a kid in its mother's milk, and that this was the reason for the prohibition against mixing milk and meat products. But it seems it may have been more than that. Robert Graves, in his classic work on mythology, The White Goddess, says that the Jews were trying to clearly delineate their religious practice from that of the goat worshippers of Dionysus, or Pan, who was a powerful deity in Palestine at the time. There was an express injunction for these worshippers to seethe a kid in its mother's milk in order to become one with Dionysus and the goat goddess, his mother. We Jews were told to do the opposite.

This prohibition means that, as well as having to take care to choose 'kosher' foods, and to make sure these have not come into contact with non-kosher foods before they reach you, you must not eat dairy dishes and meat dishes at the same meal. Furthermore you cannot use the same plates or cutlery for dairy foods as you do for meat-based foods. So you need two sets of dishes and cutlery for everyday use. And because Passover requires the use of special crockery and cutlery too, two other complete sets are kept for this occasion. Some Orthodox Jewish families build two kitchen sinks, and have two stoves and preparation areas for milk and meat and, more rarely, may even have two kitchens.

Fish and eggs are neither meat nor milk—they're neutral or pareve so you can combine them with either milk or meat. Meat and fish used in Jewish cooking must be from an approved part of the animal, and all traces of blood must be removed by washing it in salt water. Kosher meat must be initially slaughtered in a way that is meant to drain the meat of blood, and to be 'kind' to the animal. This is done under the supervision of a rabbi or the Beth Din, the Rabbinic Court of Law.

All other food must not have come into contact with forbidden foods, and Orthodox Jews will eat only grocery items that have been certified by the Beth Din.

The Holy Days and Festivals

shabbos—The sabbath

Shabbos, extending from Friday at sunset to Saturday at sunset, is the day of rest, when it is forbidden to do any work. Over the years Rabbis have argued about what God actually meant when he said not to work. They decided that besides the obvious, he meant us not to drive a car, not to turn on the electricity (or the gas), not to carry money or a handkerchief; in short, to avoid any secular activity that would take us away from our solemn duty to devote the whole day to family and prayer. The Shabbos meal is held on Friday evenings, and is a focus of Jewish life. Two candles are lit by the mother, to mark the beginning of the Holy Day, a prayer is spoken over the flames, and the family sits down to a traditional meal of chicken broth, gefillte fish, and the egg loaf called challah. The challah is blessed, as is the Sabbath wine, and the family sits around the table, seeing each other's faces through the candlelight.

purim (march)

At Purim, the Book of Esther is read. This tells the story of a beautiful Jewish girl called Esther who married the King of Persia at a time when Judah was part of the Persian empire, and foiled the evil plans of the wicked Haman, who wished to kill the Jews. As children we dressed up at Purim as characters from the Haggadah (the part of Jewish traditional literature not concerned with the religious Law), and there was always an overflow of beautiful Queen Esthers. Hamantashen are eaten, which are triangular pastries in the shape of Haman's hat, filled with poppy seeds or jam.

pesach—passover (april)

In my parents' home, Passover was the most important festival—it is a festival of freedom, a celebration of the exodus from slavery in Egypt. The evening meal on the eve of Passover is called a Seder, which is a banquet interspersed with prayers from the Haggadah. Ritual symbolic foods are cooked, such as hard-boiled eggs in salt water to symbolise life's tears of sadness, and the egg as the hope of overcoming life's burden.

On Passover, unleavened bread or matzos are eaten and leavened bread is forbidden. Dishes with matzo meal abound—it is used in cakes and pancakes and in the matzo balls (kneidlach) that float in chicken broth. By the end of the week-long festival, enough matzos have been eaten so as not to miss them for even a minute of the ensuing year, until the next Passover comes around.

Yom Kippur (september/october)

This is the Day of Atonement, when once a year we Jews fast for a night and the following day to think about our sins. This is a very solemn day. If we atone well, we are inscribed in the Book of Life, and can live another year. Kreplach, or Jewish dim sims, are eaten on the night before the fast, and are feasted on the day after to break the fast.

Channukah (december)

Channukah is the Festival of Lights, commemorating the successful resistance of Judah Maccabee and his followers to the Seleucids in 165 BC. Jews eat potato cakes (latkes) and jam doughnuts (ponchkes) at this time. The idea is to fry foods in oil, remembering the oil that miraculously lit the lamps for eight days and eight nights.

There are some other major and many minor festivals, but those I've described are the ones associated with the recipes you'll find in this book.

That's the theory—now for the practice.

I had never lived in a way that followed all the Jewish rules about food, the rules of Kashrus. My parents came to Australia in 1950, after the war in Poland had destroyed much of the Jewish community of their birth, and the life and tradition it embodied. Others came through the war strengthened in their resolve to keep the faith. My parents had lost everything, and never regained the strength to re-establish the culture they had left behind.

At Seder (the Passover evening feast meal), my father sat at the head of the table, rushing through the prayers so he could get to the part that required the eating of the soup, or the chicken or the cakes. These courses were punctuated by prayers reminding us how God helped us out of Egypt, which my father embellished with challenges to the Almighty to show him a miracle or two and then he would believe, but not until then. This religious bravado was combined with a real affection for the food, the songs, the memories and, for him, the pain of being Jewish.

So, to write a Jewish cookbook—a vast tradition of food, I thought. Where was my mother now that I needed her? She died more than 20 years before I started writing this book. But there were plenty of others to ask, and other books to consult.

Jewish cooking is more of a delicious idea than a fact, given that it's a peasant food from a time when food was scarce and limited. The trouble was that in the east of Poland, in the west of Russia, and all those cold places where the Ashkenazi Jews found themselves, there was very little money and, accordingly, not very much in the way of food to cook.

A chicken might be available, because although the Jews were not allowed to own land, a few chickens could scrape their way around any old backyard. (There is a Jewish folk saying that goes 'When a Jewish farmer eats a chicken, one of them is sick.')

Beef was much harder to come by, and very expensive. But eggs and potatoes and cabbage and a couple of carrots with an onion, now you're talking…A bit of oil or chicken fat, and some fruit and sugar and flour…some fish when there was money…that's the basis for a cultural cuisine which was pretty damn threadbare once you looked closely. Luckily, Sephardic Jews from the Middle East, North Africa and the subcontinent brought their rich and exotic cuisine to the rescue. Today, Jewish food in Australia draws from both groups, although the majority of recipes in this book are from the shtetls of Eastern Europe.

why there is no pork in this book

The first ham I ever ate was given to me by my Jewish mother. She made me ham sandwiches and sometimes even bacon and eggs. Mother was what you might call a rebellious type. She talked fondly of her uncle in Poland who was an Apikoros. This is the Yiddish name given to someone who has learned their theology and religious laws very well and, after living with the traditions and moral codes, rejects them all. (Apparently from the Greek philosopher Epicurus 341 BC–270 BC.) Apikorsus means scepticism, or heresy. (See Leo Rosten's The Joy of Yiddish, Penguin, 1972.) It is a far superior category to simple ignorance.

Mother often talked about this uncle who cut off his beard and not only rode his bike on Saturdays—a clear breaking of the Sabbath—but gave her ham sandwiches as well. It was probably this story that stimulated me to buy a pork pie once on Yom Kippur, but I couldn't bring myself to eat it.

Jews are not supposed to eat pigs because, although pigs have cloven feet, they are somewhat remiss at chewing their food, and so are off limits. And it is believed that, given the infestations to which pigs are prone in a humid climate, the prohibition against pork must have had a public health function. If it was a real matter of life and death, and pork chops were the only available food, then I suppose a little problem about chewing habits might be overlooked.

I have heard that the world's first kosher pig is being considered. This is the Babiroussa wild pig which lives in the forest and on the shores of some of the Indonesian islands and the Moluccas. Its diet is fruit and grass, and it has a set of fine tusks, whence it gets the name 'pig deer'. Israeli pig farmers are facing attempts in their parliament, the Knesset, to have pork banned, and have supported consideration of this animal as a replacement. Dayan Isaac Berger, who belongs to the London Beth Din, the chief Rabbi's court, has said:

'No-one has anything against pigs. The young ones seem gorgeous. If they had cloven feet and chewed the cud they would be acceptable. If anyone was able to produce a pig to fit the bill, then I think they would make a mint.'

I know what Rabbi Berger means about young pigs being gorgeous. I'll never forget when my dad took me to the Royal Melbourne Show and we saw a mother pig with thirteen babies, all pushing and climbing over each other to get at a teat. The mother was so pink and patient. I knew that Jews didn't like pigs, but I secretly thought that these ones were lovely. I was glad we couldn't eat them.

I just wanted to pat them.

crustaceans

Besides the ban on pig meat, there are sea creatures that we cannot eat. The rules are that we can only eat these animals if they have scales and fins. Anything you can think of must conform to both. So crustaceans are out, and oysters and other shellfish, and octopus, and most of the ingredients of a good marinara or bouillabaisse.

My mother decided to cook a lobster in Paris, just after the war. She had seen these creatures in the fish markets and in the windows of some of the best restaurants, places where a refugee working and living in one room could not afford to dine.

So she bought a lobster, to my father's surprise, and climbed the four flights to the room where they lived, the creature wrapped loosely in newspaper. She felt it move in her basket, and once a raspy claw hung over the edge, feeling its way in panic.

But Mother was panicking more. She flew in the door, put a large pot of water to boil on the stove, and contemplated the creature wrestling out of the newspapers, its whole orange body by now emerging from the basket. At this point she was ready to call a truce, to admit defeat, to keep the creature as a pet in the bath but, remembering the wages she had just spent on the meal, she took a breath and a broom handle and cornered the lobster, edging it this way and that towards the stove, like a fencer. When it was cornered, she threw a towel over it, scooped it up and dropped it into the pot, recoiling from the hardness of the claws and the strangeness of its cold touch.

Mama put the lid on the pot, but it fought that, so she placed the iron on top and was so upset that she sat outside on the balcony and read a paper, trying not to think of death by boiling.

There are rules about the kinds of food we can eat, but also about the way the food is killed. We are not allowed to eat an animal that is sick or has been maimed, or to eat an animal that has been shot, or hunted down. Certainly, slowly boiling them alive is not considered humane. Mama was taking risks again.

She heard a noise from within the room, but was too scared to look. She waited for a few minutes before she drew the curtain to see that the lid of the pot had been pushed off and the creature was no longer inside. A valiant lobster was making its way through the door, left ajar in the heat of the arrival, and my parents' dinner climbed down the stairs to the Paris streets, to freedom.

antipodean cuisine

I rang my sister Amanda's father-in-law to ask whether seals were kosher. 'Seals?' he said. They don't have seals in Poland.

'You know, they're mammals, they live half in water and half on land.'

'The rules are very straightforward: if they are sea creatures they must have scales and fins. If they are land creatures they must have cloven hooves and chew the cud, and they have to chew all the time.'

'Seals have flippers, not hooves,' I countered. 'On the other hand their flippers are a bit like fins, but they don't have scales.'

'No, you can't eat a seal, Ramona.'

Later I thought about the lack of flexibility, and the geocentricity of the rule; what about Jews in Lapland, or in the Antarctic, or even in Australia? I rang him again.

'Kangaroos? What about kangaroos?'

'We can't eat anything with claws. That's not including birds of course.'

'Then, can we eat penguins?'

'You want to eat a penguin? There's a list in Leviticus, chapter 11, verse 2, there you can check whether you can eat a penguin. But I don't think you can eat a penguin.'

'But this list was made up in the Middle East. How can it have an opinion on penguins and seals, or even kangaroos?'

'Because the Maker told us this is what we could eat, and these other things we couldn't. You think the Maker didn't remember that he made the seals and the penguins and the kangaroos? He made them after all, but it's just that we can't eat them.'

I ate some kangaroo once, cooked in a deep pit, in its own skin. I had not seen the hunt, because deep in the desert, this was men's business, as was the cooking of the meat and its distribution. It tasted like roast lamb, with the grey coals still on the outside.

The great evolutionary theorist Charles Darwin formed a club while a student at Cambridge. It was really a drinking club, but part of the fun was the 'eating of strange flesh'. Each week they would try to catch and cook something that hadn't been eaten by humans before, or at least by Englishmen. That's how the London Zoo started, of course—to provide exotic beasts for English gentlefolk to eat. The lions and the tigers and the giraffes all went under the silver knives and forks of the gentry.

When we eat strange flesh we are crossing boundaries—those of our own making and those imposed on us.

Mother bought the lobster in defiance. She was at war with her Maker. We went to Healesville Wildlife Sanctuary once, where she sized up the kangaroos, and took a side glance at an emu leg. Mother was an omnivore, an eater of strange flesh. If she were still alive I would take her 600km (375 miles) south-west of Alice Springs, where we would dig for honey ants, biting off their golden abdomens for the rich, sweet honey—truly strange flesh for you, Mother—a boundary of thorax and abdomen and six legs to cross, not even dreamt of in Leviticus.

What was never dreamt of by me was that after I turned fifty, I would be establishing a kosher kitchen, with two sets of dishes, cutlery, cooking utensils and pots and pans, and becoming a regular customer at the local kosher butchers. I had not found religion after all these years, but my younger daughter had fallen in love with a young man who was an Orthodox Jew in outlook and practice. And which Jewish mother could cope with not being able to feed her whole family, together under the one roof, from her very own kitchen? When they married, my son-in-law supervised the transformation, and I was not present on the day a Rabbi with a blow torch arrived, but apparently all the required steps were taken and now everyone eats at Bubba's (grandmother's) house.

so here are the recipes, some that i learned from my mother, one from my father, and some that others have told me as I sat in their kitchens and watched them cooking, talking to them with my tape recorder on. Some are from Poland, Russia, Hungary and Austria; some from the Levant and the Middle East, which has seen the rise of Israeli cooking, a cuisine similar to that of our Arab cousins.

But no matter what you are cooking, the secret is to set aside the afternoon, make the kitchen warm if it is winter, cool if it is summer, pull up a few chairs for children, family and guests, and chop and knead and boil while you talk.

'Tell me a story about your life,' I would say as my mother rolled out the pastry.

'Would you like to hear about when you were little?' I offer my daughters a seat.

'Come and stand on a chair and help me cook,' I invite my eldest granddaughter, 'and I'll tell you a story'.

Here, dear reader, pull up a chair, watch me cook, and listen to a few stories…

entrées

The general idea is to cover the table with food so that there is no room for creeping anxiety about whether everyone will get enough to eat, so it is not unusual to have several entrées in small dishes on the table, and for the diners to take a little of each. Pickled herring strips need no preparation, nor do carrots and celery used to dip into the various dishes. But the best thing to eat with any of these is bagels—boiled or baked, covered with poppy seeds, sesame seeds or plain—just as long as they are fresh and preferably warm.

chopped eggs and onions

Serves 6–8

2 large onions
12 hard-boiled eggs
110g (4oz) butter, melted
salt and black pepper to taste
parsley sprigs

Chop the onions and combine with the eggs, still chopping until the mixture is very fine.
Combine the butter with the eggs and the onions seasoning with salt and pepper.
Garnish with parsley and serve with table water biscuits or matzos.

stuffed Hard-boiled eggs

Serves 6

8 large hard-boiled eggs
110g (4oz) unsalted butter, melted
3 tablespoons chopped fresh dill
2 tablespoons cream
2 tablespoons chopped fresh parsley
2 tablespoons chopped fresh chives
1 teaspoon sweet paprika
salt and black pepper to taste
breadcrumbs for garnish
grated cheese for garnish

Shell the eggs and halve them along their longest axis.
Choose the 12 best halves and scoop out the yolks.
To make the stuffing add these yolks to the remaining eggs, and chop very finely. Add the rest of the ingredients. Divide the mixture amongst the reserved halves, sprinkle with breadcrumbs and cheese, and dot each egg with a little unsalted butter. Bake in a hot oven for 10 minutes.

mushroom blintzes

Makes 12

Blintzes are simply fine pancakes with either sweet or savoury fillings. With mushrooms or potatoes, they become entrées—with cheese or cherries, they're dessert. They are great because you can make the pancakes ahead of time and freeze them individually, bringing them out with great aplomb when unexpected guests arrive. But most of my unexpected guests would be happy to sit in the kitchen and watch me make the pancakes in a theatrical way. Then they can be enlisted to clean up.

Batter:
3 eggs
1 cup (170g/6oz) plain flour
1 cup (250ml/8fl oz) milk
butter for frying

Beat eggs till light and fluffy, add sifted flour and beat again. Add milk and stir.
Leave to stand for 10 minutes so that batter will thicken.

Filling:
1 cup (about 110g/4oz) mushrooms
30g (1oz) butter
1 medium onion, grated
1 cup (140g/5oz) grated cheese
salt and pepper to taste

Slice the mushrooms. Melt the butter in a frying pan, add the mushrooms and onion, and cover and cook over a low heat for about 5 minutes. Remove from heat, add the cheese, salt and pepper. Set aside.
Heat 1 teaspoon of butter in a clean frying pan until hot.
Add enough batter to finely cover the pan. Fry on one side then the other.
Put aside on a warm plate. Repeat until all the batter has been used, melting a fresh teaspoon of butter in the pan before pouring each new pancake. To form the blintzes, place 2 dessertspoons of filling into the centre of each pancake, fold each one inwards at two opposite sides, then roll up into parcels.

gechakte Laber
(chopped liver)

'At fancy restaurants, they might make a fuss about the paté and the terrines,' said my mother, 'but don't feel put down, remember it's really gechakte laber—old-fashioned chopped liver.'

1 tablespoon chicken fat (schmaltz), available from some delicatessens
2 medium onions, finely sliced and 1 clove garlic, crushed
1 teaspoon salt and 1 teaspoon pepper
450g (1lb) chicken livers
3 large hard-boiled eggs
pinch of nutmeg

Melt the fat in a pan. Add onions, garlic, salt and pepper and fry lightly for about 3–4 minutes or until golden brown. Add chicken livers and cook for 10 minutes on low heat. Cool slightly. Place in a food processor, with the eggs and nutmeg and blend for 30 seconds to 1 minute.
Leave purée to stand in a bowl in the fridge until needed. For a consistency more like the chopped liver my mother made, forget the processor and take to the mixture with a knife on a chopping board.
Chopped liver can be served in small individual bowls as an entrée, or spread on bread or biscuits as a snack.

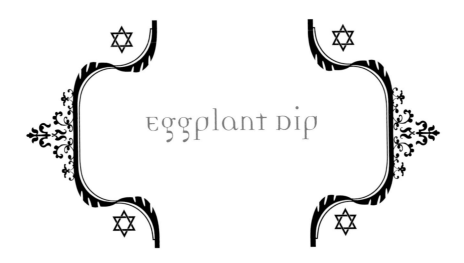

eggplant dip

When I was at Jewish Sunday School, my teacher said the sages believed that the manna that fell from heaven to keep the Israelites alive for forty years in the desert, was actually eggplant. And that the reason why the Israelites didn't get sick of it was that you could prepare it in so many different ways. Including this one.

1 large eggplant (aubergine)
1 onion, finely chopped and 1 clove garlic, crushed
½ teaspoon salt and ½ teaspoon black pepper
1 teaspoon lemon juice
1 tablespoon olive oil or mayonnaise

Halve the eggplant. Place both halves into a baking dish and bake for 35–40 minutes at about 220°C (450°F), until the skin chars. Scoop out the flesh from the skin and mash it. When cool, add the onion, garlic, salt, pepper and lemon juice, then the oil or mayonnaise, and serve as a dip with biscuits or bread.

knishes

Makes about 20

Knishes are small, semi-circular baked pastries, usually stuffed with either a mushroom or cheese filling. They are related to the Russian pastries called piroshki, which can also be served as 'finger food' or with soup. According to an internet search, knishes are 'America's newest comfort food'. You can still buy them on the streets of New York, much as you have been able to do since the turn of the last century.

Dough:
2 cups (340g/12oz) plain flour and 1 teaspoon baking powder
pinch of salt and black pepper
3 eggs, plus one egg, beaten
6 tablespoons oil
water as required

Sift together the flour, baking powder, salt and pepper.
Slowly add the beaten eggs to a well you've made in the centre of the dry ingredients.
Add the oil and mix in a little water to form a dough.
(It should have a similar consistency to scone dough.)
Knead the dough until it's beautifully smooth, with no cracks.

Cheese filling:
2 large onions, fried
2 eggs
¼ cup (60ml/2fl oz) pure (double) cream
500g (1lb 2oz) cottage cheese
salt and black pepper to taste
½ teaspoon paprika
Beat all ingredients together.

or Mushroom filling:
500g (1lb 2oz) mushrooms, thinly sliced
1 large onion, chopped
60g (2oz) butter
1 hard-boiled egg
¼ cup (60ml/2fl oz) pure (double) cream
salt and pepper to taste
breadcrumbs

Sauté mushrooms and onion in butter until tender. Stir in the chopped egg,
salt, pepper and cream and add enough breadcrumbs to make a filling of slightly thick consistency.

Preheat oven to 180°C (350°F). Roll the dough out thinly.
Use a cup to cut out circles roughly 5cm (2 inches) in diameter and put a spoonful of either filling in the
centre of each one. Lift the edges of the pastry circle towards the centre to join over the filling. Pinch the
edges together, brush with beaten egg, and bake in a moderate oven until brown—about 15 minutes.

My sister Amanda's mother-in-law invited me to their Seder some years ago, when my children were going to their father's family. It is seen as a good deed, or mitzvah to invite a stranger, or one who is alone, to the celebration. She had spent many days preparing the meal, which began with the gefillte fish. She served each person a piece with a slice of carrot on the top, and a dab of horseradish. Joe, her elder son, looked at the ceiling, taking a deep breath. 'None for me, Mother.'

'What did you say?'

'No gefillte fish for me.'

'Are you sick or something?'

'No, I'm not sick. I just don't want any fish.'

'Did you taste it, is there something wrong with the fish?'

'No, Mum. You know I don't eat gefillte fish. I never eat gefillte fish.'

'I didn't know you don't like fish.'

'Mum, I tell you every year, every Passover, that I don't like the fish, every year for 43 years, and every year you make a fuss.'

'But when you were a little boy, I gave you a piece of gefillte fish every day. You never said a word.'

Joe took the plate and added another spoonful of horseradish, the bitter herb.

gefillte fish
(fish balls)

Gefillte fish is a fine example of the essential economy of traditional Jewish cooking. Fish was expensive in Poland, and so the good homemaker had to be careful to make sure it went a long way. This dish can also be found in the traditional food of non-Jews in the northern European countries—people in places inland from the sea all had recipes to make freshwater fish more flavoursome. Among the Sephardic Jews who live on the Mediterranean seaboard where saltwater fish is available, this recipe is virtually unknown. These fish balls are a combination of fish (several types to be authentic), eggs, seasoning, matzo meal and almond meal, and a taste of sweetness.

Gefillte fish is the crowning achievement of the cook. A woman (for Jewish cooks are almost always women) can be judged by her gefillte fish: does it come apart after cooking; is it too sweet or not sweet enough; is it too fishy; are the pieces too small (there is hardly anything that is ever too big); has she been generous enough with the ingredients? Traditionally, it is the entrée to Seder, the Passover feast.

Stock:
2 onions, cut into quarters
1 green capsicum (green pepper), diced
3 carrots, sliced
4 celery stalks, sliced
2 litres (3½ pints) water
fish heads, bones and skin (ask the fishmonger to keep them after filleting)
1 tablespoon salt
½ tablespoon freshly ground pepper
handful of chopped parsley and 1 bay leaf

Place all the stock ingredients in a large pot, and bring to the boil while you make the fish balls.

Fish:
2kg (4lbs 8oz) murray perch (filleted),
500g (1lb 2oz) carp (filleted)
500g (1lb 2oz) white fish (filleted)
1 tablespoon salt
2 medium onions, grated
6 eggs
1 tablespoon olive oil
1 teaspoon sugar
½ cup (60g/2oz) matzo meal
½ cup (60g/2oz) almond meal

Finely chop the fish, or grind it if you have the equipment. Add the rest of the ingredients.
Mix well with your hands, and then, wetting your hands so the mixture doesn't stick, form mixture into oval-shaped balls, roughly 4cm x 8cm (1½ inches x 3 inches). Carefully place the balls into simmering stock. Cook slowly for about 2 hours. When the balls are cooked, remove them from the stock and cool.
Strain the stock, remove the vegetables and chill until set.
Serve the fish cold with a carrot slice, a dab of horseradish and some jellied fish stock.

You can also fry the fish balls in hot oil after they have cooled, and serve this
as an alternative to the boiled fish balls.

gullah, petcha, fusnogge
what's in a name?
(calf's-foot jelly)
Serves 8–10

Someone read a draft of this book and exclaimed—'What? No gullah?'
'What's gullah?' I said.
'Everyone knows,' she went on, 'My mother eats it but I can't stand it.'
I can't remember my mother ever cooking gullah (or petcha or fusnogge as it's also known), or maybe she never
made me eat it. She was a woman ahead of her time in many ways. So I rang my sister. She is sitting in her kitchen
with her husband and a friend.
'Ramona wants to know what gullah is?'
Immediately she tells me they're pulling faces. 'They know what it is but they say they hate it. No one from our
generation likes it.'
But in the interest of completeness, here, for your enjoyment is gullah…calf's-foot jelly.

2 calf's feet
1 large onion, peeled
2 cloves garlic, peeled
3 bay leaves
1 teaspoon black peppercorns
salt and pepper to taste
2 tablespoons lemon juice
3 hard-boiled eggs

Put the feet in a flameproof casserole dish, cover with cold water, bring to the boil and then simmer for
10 minutes. Skim off the froth and add the onion, garlic, bay leaves, peppercorns, and salt and pepper.
Simmer for about 3 hours until the meat and gristle come away from the bone and the liquid is reduced
by half. Remove the bones. Lift the meat out and cut into cubes.
Strain the liquid into a bowl and return it to the casserole dish with lemon juice and meat.
Bring it to the boil again. Remove from heat, pour into a jelly dish, add slices of egg in a layer on top and
refrigerate until set. Serve garnished with slices of lemon and parsley.

LOX
(sliced salmon)

Serves 4–6

What could be more perfect on a fresh bagel than cream cheese and lox, or sliced salmon?

1.5kg (3lb 6oz) salmon; fresh, centre cut,
2 bunches fresh dill
¼ cup (60g/2oz) salt and ¼ cup (60g/2oz) sugar
2 tablespoons white peppercorns
1 lemon cut into wedges and black pepper for garnish

Place half of the fish, skin side down, in a deep dish. Place 1½ bunches of dill over the fish. Sprinkle dry ingredients over dill. Top with the other half of the fish, skin side up. Cover with foil. Weigh down with a cutting board and a weight on top. My father says in Poland they used a brick, but something from inside the house will do—perhaps a volume of the Encyclopaedia Judaica.
Refrigerate for 48–72 hours, turning the salmon and basting every 12 hours with the accumulated juices.
When ready to serve, remove the fish from the marinade and pat dry.
Slice salmon thinly on the diagonal and serve. Cut up the remaining half bunch of dill and sprinkle over the fish, together with black pepper.

avocado Dip

How did they grow avocados in the shtetl? They didn't. This is a Sephardic dish (sometimes disguised as guacamole)
that finds favour everywhere. In the shtetl they hardly ever had oranges, unless someone imported them from far away.
The first time Mama saw a banana, she was on a boat bound for Australia.
She had to wait some time to finally meet a Queensland avocado.

2 ripe avocados
6 hard-boiled eggs
1 large onion, chopped and 1 clove garlic, crushed
salt and black pepper to taste
½ teaspoon ground chilli powder
2 tablespoons vinegar or lemon juice

Mash the avocado with the eggs. Add the onion, garlic, seasonings and vinegar.
Serve as a dip with biscuits or bread.

Herring salad

Serves 6

The kids at school were very judgemental about the food we brought for lunch, and nothing would be more sure to provoke their ire than herring salad. It was universally despised. We learned to demand 'normal food' and fit in. But, as usual, I took it too far…

3 onions, chopped and 1 green apple, grated
1 teaspoon sugar and 1 tablespoon lemon juice
4 pickled herrings
2 cups (500ml/16 fl oz) sour cream

Combine onions, apple and sugar and add the lemon juice. Cut the herrings into cubes, combine the lot with sour cream and serve.

I had come home one day in early December of

my Grade Two year and had asked if I could take a tea towel to school.

'Are you going to cook something, Rivkele?'

'No, it's for a play.'

'What kind of a play?'

'It's just a play about a lady with a baby and she wears a tea towel around her head. It's nothing, really.'

I had neglected to tell my mother that for the whole year I had been going to Christian religious instruction classes. This was because I had heard about my parents' difficulties with those who didn't understand Jews, and I thought it best that I act undercover. I felt a pang of regret as the other Jewish kids filed out each week for a session with the Rabbi, but I liked the stories about Jesus, especially the miracles. They seemed more spectacular than Moses'. I particularly liked the one about the loaves and fishes. So I learned the Lord's Prayer, and my hand went up first every time when we were asked about the Good Samaritan and the women at the well. No wonder that when it came to choosing a responsible Mary, they looked no further than me.

'So what does this lady with the baby and the tea towel on her head actually do?'

'She just sits around, in a zoo.'

'You mean there are animals with this baby?'

'A couple.'

'Would this be a Christmas play by any chance?'

'Yeah, maybe that's what it is.'

'Do they know you are Jewish, Ramona?'

She always called me Ramona when she was really serious. So I had to explain about the safety aspects of religious instruction classes and that, as she had survived by pretending to be Christian, I had thought that learning to be one was a pretty good idea.

She took me up to the school the next morning, to the headmaster's office, where she blew my cover. He was aghast. Where were they going to find a replacement Mary at this late stage? They didn't have an understudy!

My mother calmed him. 'Don't forget, sir, that Mary was one of us!' The authenticity cheered them both. And on the morning of the play, the local Reverend patted my head as I walked by him with the tea towel on my head and the doll in my arms, and my mother stood in the audience with a distant look on her face, and a tear in her eye.

soups

Soup is absolutely essential to the meal—a digestive balance, a healthful preventative of illness, a sign of a strong, warm home, of love embodied. Unlike the Italians, we didn't usually eat it with bread. There was so much more to come, and filling up on bread was a sign of ingratitude.Chicken broth on Friday nights, barley soup or borscht during the week, cold borscht for summer—there was never a time when soup was not called for.

cherry
soup

Serves 6

*In my mind's eye, the Polish landscape of my parents' birth is always covered with snow. I used to complain of walk-
ing through the rain to school, and would be met with stories of brave and obedient children trudging miles to school
through drifts of snow in the weak light of morning, and then back again through the afternoon darkness. Soup was
on the stove to take the chill out of your bones, and you could warm your hands against the plate.*

*There was no fun in the stories they told me, and since fun meant summer, I had forgotten that there must have
been summer, and summer soups. This soup was not one my mother made, but other mothers made it from the stone
fruit available in a Polish summer. It was served chilled, with sour cream and fresh mint, in the heat of the day.*

450g (1lb) cherries, halved and stoned
200g (7oz) pears, peeled and sliced
310g (11oz) plums, halved and stoned (blood plums give a good result)
60g (2oz) sugar
¼ teaspoon salt
1 teaspoon ground cinnamon
juice and rind of 1 lemon
1.2 litres (2 pints) water

Put everything except the cornflour in a large saucepan and bring to the boil, stirring occasionally.
Simmer until the fruit is tender.
Mix in a blender until smooth, then add the cornflour, which has been
mixed to a paste with a little of the soup.
Bring to the boil again, lower the heat, and simmer until the soup thickens slightly.
Add more sugar to taste.
Cool until ready to serve. Add a dessertspoonful of sour cream and a dash of chopped mint
from the garden to each bowl.

The image of my parents walking through the snow

to school was shattered one day when my mother told us that my father lived in 'School Street'. How could it have been so far to walk when you lived in the same street as the school? My father was furious. He went away to another school, not the one in his street, but another one, and it was very far away!

My father's first day at school was in winter. His birthday is in November and he would have just turned seven. His mother, a widow with four children, packed a lunch for her youngest son, and put it in a bag for him to carry.

My father walked up the road in the snow, where he was met by a goat who was very interested in his lunch. When you're seven, he says, if a goat asks for your lunch, you don't argue. He turned in his tracks and headed home, where his mother was surprised to see him so soon.

'Why didn't you go to school?' she asked.

'Well, the goat wanted my lunch so I let him go to school.'

Borscht
(beetroot soup)

Serves 8

Borscht can be served steaming hot in winter, or as a cold summer soup. It is a fine example of the Jewish nomads' tendency to absorb the cuisine of the region in which they found themselves, and to adapt it to their dietary laws. As it is forbidden to mix milk and meat products, each meal must be clearly designated as 'milk' or 'meat', and the food to be served adjusted accordingly. Borscht is a Russian staple, and was quickly taken up by both Russian and Polish Jews. It can be made using a beef stock and served as a winter soup with a boiled potato steaming in the centre of the plate, or as a pure vegetable soup that goes with a dairy-based, or milchich meal, served with sour cream.

The most delicious way to eat it is—dare I say it—as the rich meat soup with a dollop of sour cream. Regarding the flagrant breaking of the dietary laws, my mother had a way of putting it: 'God and I have an arrangement,' she used to say, 'I don't ask him what he eats, and he doesn't ask me what I eat.'

1kg (2lbs 4oz) beetroot, topped and tailed
juice of 3 lemons
2 litres (4 pints) vegetable or chicken stock
(to be Kosher: if using the chicken stock you can't serve with yoghurt or sour cream)
3 small potatoes, peeled and diced
1 large onion, coarsely chopped
1 large bunch of fresh dill roughly chopped,
2 tablespoons sugar
pepper to taste and 2 teaspoons salt
Sour cream or yoghurt (about 1 dessertspoonful per person)

Peel the beetroots and place them whole into a large pot. Pour over the juice of a lemon and add 3-4 cups water and stock to cover. Place the pot over medium heat and cook for 40 minutes until the beetroot is tender. The beetroot is cooked when the flesh is tender enough for a knife to cut through to the other side without getting stuck. Remove the beetroot from the liquid and cut into small pieces.

Put the cut beetroot into a large saucepan with the potato, onion and dill. Add sugar and remaining lemon juice. Season with freshly ground pepper and salt. Cover and return to the stove. Bring to the boil then simmer for another hour. Blend if you want a smooth texture, or serve it in a more rustic fashion. Serve hot or chill until icy cold. Serve with a spoonful of sour cream and a sprinkle of dill.

winter borscht
(meat and vegetable soup)

Serves 8

If you still know people who eat meat, this warming winter version of borscht is especially good for those in need of iron, or the naturally and boisterously carnivorous.

1.5 litres (2 pints 14fl oz) water
1kg (2lbs 4oz) chuck steak, diced
2 lamb shanks
1kg (2lbs 4oz) beetroot, peeled and sliced
half a small cabbage, shredded
2 carrots
1 large onion
2 celery stalks
1 green capsicum (green pepper) and 1 red capsicum (red pepper)
1 potato
2–3 cloves garlic, minced
salt and pepper to taste
juice of 1 lemon
1 teaspoon sugar
oregano to taste

Bring water to the boil, then add meat and shanks. Cook over a medium flame until scum forms at the top—skim this off. Parboil sliced beetroot to soften; grate all the vegetables (including the softened beetroot) and add to the meat. Season with garlic, salt, pepper, lemon juice, sugar and oregano. Cover and cook on a low heat for 2 hours. Serve hot.

MENA SOLOMON LIVES WITH HER HUSBAND DAVID in a ground-floor flat in Brisbane, south of the river, among weary weatherboards, warehouses and factories. It's a Sunday morning in September and 30°C. We have decided to make borscht, because Mena Solomon was born Mena Borscht, and it seemed like an omen.

She is a tiny, attractive woman of 83, long a community stalwart and a force in all the major organisations; she was even a founder of the Jewish Girl Guide troop in 1926. She kisses me, on our first meeting, and holds my hand as she takes me into her kitchen. It's bright and clean and homely.

Mena was born in China, in Harbin. Her family had fled the pogroms that beset Odessa in the first ten years of this century. She is cooking her borscht, which is pareve (neutral), meaning it can be served with either milk or meat dishes.

'It's my own recipe. I made it up and I'll tell you why. My mother came from Rumania and she used to make either a hot borscht or a cold borscht. She'd make the cold borscht with beetroot, potato and onions, and when it got cool, she'd beat up a couple of eggs and put them in. For hot borscht she'd do it with a shank. Then I got the idea of my own that I could have her cold borscht hot or cold, so I don't put egg in it unless I particularly make a cold borscht for the summer. We like cold borscht in the summer, but more often than not in the winter months we have it without meat, but I use the pareve chicken stock and that gives it a lovely flavour as well.

'When you put the beetroot in, you have to keep the flavour in it, so you add lemon juice, and a little bit of sugar, otherwise the beetroot boils out and it's a 'nothing' colour. Then you put in some salt and pepper, and that brings the flavour out. I don't grate the beetroot first, I let it cook and grate it afterwards, and then put in the potato and the onions.'

Mena and her mother came to Brisbane in 1913 after living in Harbin for four years. Her father was a shoemaker, and after much convincing by her mother, he took a slow boat and came out first. He had no idea if he was going to America, or Australia, and simply got off following other Jewish families. He spoke Yiddish, Russian and a little Chinese, but no English. He worked with a pick and shovel on the roads and went to English classes before getting a job in a shoe shop again.

'All Mum wanted to do when she got here was to go out into the country. Where she came from in Kishinev, they used to make their own wine—do you want to try some? We make it too—David and I and our two grandchildren made this.'

Mena is brandishing some of the wine she has made even though it is only ten in the morning. It is very sweet and very good.

'It's a sweet one, very sweet, and all it's got in it is muscatels and shiraz, not another thing. I remember when my mother used to do it and the boys used to get into the tub and stamp on the grapes, that's how far back it used to be.'

Mena takes the scum off the top of the soup, and then when the beets are softer, removes them, slicing them into small strips.

'Now I'm dicing a potato to put into the borscht. I'll put some diced onion in, too, now—I don't want to put it in too early. And now I'll put in a little bit of salt.'

'We had a shochet who used to come and kill our chickens. We would pluck them under the house. We'd each put a scarf around our hair and we'd have to pluck them—so with these and with the meat the kosher butcher provided, we maintained our Jewish life.'

Mena's husband, David, enters the kitchen.

'As you see I am a product of 54 years of cooking, so I'm not bad, am I? She hasn't poisoned me yet.'

Mena is showing me the pareve chicken stock she uses—chicken stock without the chicken. It's called Vita and comes from Israel.

Before I left, the beetroot had been shredded and put back into the soup, and Mena had brought out some photographs. One was of the committee of the Deshon Street Synagogue in 1919, standing outside a weatherboard schule. Another was of her father, Michael Borscht, working with a pick and shovel in the Brisbane heat. The faces of the Girl Guides walking to the top of One Tree Hill in stockings and high heels in 1926, or of the young matrons in 1947 could have been found in Eastern Europe, or on the streets of Odessa, if it weren't for the tropical banana palms swaying in the breeze.

kasha soup
(barley soup)

Serves 6

I hated this soup. The night my father showed me photographs of the concentration camps, we had barley soup steaming away in our plates, the Sabbath candles on the table. The tablecloth was white. My father gave me the book, a souvenir from an anniversary of the Warsaw ghetto uprising. I saw children with hollow eyes and sticks for legs. They had no underpants. One of them smiled as he sat up on a tray waiting to be put into an oven.

One day in winter I was old enough to cook it up. Having come to trust this soup's qualities of hearth and home (and its delicious taste) I gave it to my children. They hated it.

My grandchildren will not thank me for including this recipe. But each generation has to suffer in its own way.

1 turnip, chopped and 2 large onions, chopped
4 medium carrots, chopped and 2 sticks celery, chopped
60g (2oz) butter or 2 tablespoons oil
2 litres (3 pints 4fl oz) water
1 cup pearl barley, soaked in water overnight
salt and pepper to taste
chopped parsley

Toss the turnip, onion and carrot in the butter or oil in a large pot, and cook with the lid on for 15 minutes, stirring occasionally. Add the water, bring to the boil, then add the barley. Cover the pot and cook on a low heat until the barley is tender (about 1–1½ hours). Add salt and pepper to taste. If the soup is too thick, you can add more water or milk. Serve with chopped parsley.

Barley and mushroom soup
Serves 6

In some families it was possible to 'redeem' barley soup by the addition of mushrooms and beef stock. You can use 300g (11oz) fresh mushrooms and add dried mushrooms to this if you like. Toss vegetables and mushrooms in oil (tossing in butter would make the soup non-kosher in this recipe), and instead of water, add beef broth.

chicken broth

Serves 8

There are far too many jokes about chicken broth, and I won't add to the overload. In the Pale of Settlement, chickens were the cheapest form of meat, and the efficient housewife would be able to use just about every part of the bird for the Sabbath meal.

Chopped liver would be the entrée, with a rich soup with matzo balls, rice or another carbohydrate added, and then the boiled meat from the broth would be removed and served after the soup with vegetables and challah.

1 large chicken
2 veal shanks
3 carrots
1 parsnip
2 stalks celery
1 onion
1 handful chopped parsley
salt and pepper to taste
1 bunch dill, chopped
2 litres (3 pints 4fl oz) water (more or less)

Boil the whole chicken with the veal shanks until the fatty scum floats to the top.
Skim it off and discard. If you have the time, put the pot of broth into the fridge overnight and lift the congealed fat off the top of the soup before bringing it to the boil and adding the vegetables.
Chop the vegetables and add them to the pot, together with salt, pepper and dill.
Lower the heat and simmer for 1½ hours. The meat can be served in the soup, or separately, as a main course with vegetables. Jewish meat cooking seems to be mainly about boiling. This may be because cheaper cuts were so old and tough that boiling was the only thing to do to make them edible.
Chicken broth can be served with noodles, rice, baked or fried dough (mandlen), matzo balls (kneidlach), or meat pastries (kreplach)—see page 58.

vegetarian chicken broth

Serves about 8

What happened to make so many of our children into born-again vegetarians? Was it the work of Animal Rights ethicist Peter Singer (who appears later in this book making ethical jam doughnuts, or ponchkes) and the vision of countless miserable chooks in tiny cages that made them turn their noses up? I couldn't believe that vegetarianism could actually exclude such a holy broth as Mama's chicken soup, but I found I had to freeze larger and larger volumes of the stuff which had not been eaten. Then I got the message. Here is a recipe from a friend who said that as a vegetarian, she had to devise a soup which she could happily cook for the Jewish holidays. According to her, this soup, when served up with matzo balls made with olive oil, passes the scrutiny of the most critical judges.

2 tablespoons olive oil
3 large leeks, chopped
1 tablespoon chopped fresh ginger
1 tablespoon chopped garlic
3 or 4 large turnips, chopped
3 or 4 large parsnips, chopped
3 or 4 large carrots, chopped
1 whole celery, chopped
2 large bunches dill and 1 bunch parsley
½ teaspoon cracked peppercorns
salt and pepper to taste
2 teaspoons honey or sugar

Heat olive oil or margarine in a big soup pot. Throw in the leeks, ginger and garlic. Cook, stirring until the leeks are transparent. Add all the vegetables except the dill and parsley. Stir the vegetables to stop them from burning, adding a little water occasionally. When the vegetables have softened a little, add the dill and parsley. Cover with water. Add salt, pepper and peppercorns. Bring to boil, turn down, taking the scum off the top, and cook for 1½ hours. Add 2 teaspoons of honey or sugar, and seasoning to taste. When the vegetables are soft (but not falling apart) and the broth tastes good, turn the soup off and strain. Serve the broth only.

κneidlach
(matzo balls)

Makes about 20

Kneidlach are traditionally served at Passover, when noodles or mandlen are forbidden because of the prohibition against using anything containing leaven.

1 small onion, chopped
2 tablespoons oil (or chicken fat)
2 eggs, lightly beaten and 1 tablespoon cold water
half bunch parsley, finely chopped
¾ cup (110g/4oz) fine matzo meal
¼ cup (30g/1oz) almond meal (optional)
salt and pepper to taste

Fry the onion in the oil or fat until golden. Remove from heat and combine with all ingredients. Let stand for
10 minutes, then form into balls. If you keep your hands wet with cold water, this will be easy. Drop them into boiling soup (see recipe for chicken broth, page 51) and cook for about 20 minutes.

Rabbi Rudolph Brasch—liberal Jew, popular author and cosmopolitan—lives in Vaucluse with a magnificent view of Sydney Harbour. Prolific in his literary output, his subjects are as diverse as the origin of sex and the origin of sport—the list is still growing since he retired from congregational work more than ten years ago.

Born and educated in Germany—'I had the best of teachers in theology and in languages'—Rabbi Brasch is a speaker with an encyclopaedic knowledge which brings him invitations to lecture from all over the world. His PhD thesis was an analysis of commentaries on the Song of Songs.

He has led liberal Jewish congregations in England, Ireland, South Africa and Australia, where he met his wife Li, who is his secretary, manager and agent. They have been inseparable for nearly 50 years.

The Braschs travel extensively on lecturing and preaching tours; once Rabbi Brasch was an 'enrichment lecturer' on a P&O cruise ship. They are inevitably researching the next book, as Rabbi Brasch says he doesn't know what he's looking for until he finds it. With no children, and a busy working schedule, they say they have no time for cooking.

'Of course,' says Rabbi Brasch, 'we have our favourite dishes in every country. We still love going to England to eat new potatoes, garden peas, roast lamb and mint sauce. In America we used to love pastrami until it went chemical!'

Of the Jewish love of food he says: 'The Jews were perhaps interested in food and eating because they had not much else to enjoy. Jews have always been very family-minded. The family really surrounds the hearth, and you know the origin of the word 'companion'? It means "together with the bread".'

'Over the years,' Li says, 'I picked up from here and there recipes that are quick, because I can't waste time. I'd much rather type a hundred pages than cook a meal. If we're going to start proofreading because the publisher has said they'll send a courier round with the proofs, that means I put on a pot of Irish stew this size (she makes a huge gesture) and we will eat that until it comes out of our ears. We don't even know we're eating it because we're not interested in food, all we want to do is read the proofs. We do it together, naturally. I read them out and he has the galleys in front of him.' Li is a small woman with bright eyes behind her glasses. Her sentences happily run into her husband's.

'But it wasn't always like this,' Rabbi Brasch is saying. 'Originally I would read aloud and she would have the proofs, and you know how you read it: "And he said, comma, quotes, comma"—well, we were proofreading and I was also preaching and taking services, of course, and one day I said "The Lord our God, comma". From then on we changed over, and that's a true story!

'Our longest meal is breakfast, not that we have much—toast and vegemite and grapefruit—but it's the longest because we do the puzzles, or we read. All the other meals are very short, one-course meals, because we really don't care—for us eating is a professional hazard, we eat at so many functions, we have so many weddings.'

'When he asked me to marry him,' Li says, 'I had to admit to him that I couldn't cook.'

'He said, "But can you type?" and I've been typing ever since. But when we have visitors I get very, very nervous because it's hit and miss with me. One day we had a bachelor Rabbi coming from the United States and I botched up every single course. Either he was very polite, or he thought it was Australian cooking, as he ate his way through it without blinking an eyelash. Such a polite man.'

'Up here in Vaucluse there was a fishmonger where I used to go to buy fish for grilling. It was getting near our Jewish New Year and he said to me "Mrs Brasch, I'm going to mince some fish for gefillte fish, and if you come in two days' time, I'll have some for you as a present—I know your New Year is coming". I couldn't say no, I picked the minced fish up but I had no cookbook. So I thought to myself, you put an egg in it, and some breadcrumbs, but I couldn't really get it to stick, so I put in more and more breadcrumbs and eventually, I managed to form these small balls. When I put them in the boiling salt water they swelled and swelled, and they ended up like footballs!'

'When my husband started to eat them he said "You know, they're not gefillte fish, they're bread balls!" I said, "Ah, let's give them a chance," so I called the cat and I dished up one ball to the cat, who relished it, and so they were gefillte fish after all!'

But Li has a secret recipe for matzo balls (kneidlach).

'It's easy, it never fails because it's one, one, one, one. One cup of coarse matzo meal—you put it in a bowl with salt, pepper and a big teaspoon of ground ginger. Mix it and—this is the secret, it has to be really boiling—add a cup of boiling water, mix that in, and then add a tablespoon of chicken fat, but I use polyunsaturated oil, and one beaten-up egg. You use enough matzo meal so that when you put your finger in it leaves an indentation, because overnight the moisture soaks up and if you make them too hard to begin with, they get too hard. You cook them for three-quarters of an hour in the soup with the lid on.'

Li says 'Having no children, we really live for each other, we are everything to one another.' She beamed at the Rabbi and then looked at me.

'Second helpings?'

The Rabbi smiles: 'A woman to show her appreciation asks for a recipe, a man to show his appreciation asks for a second helping!'

mandlen

(baked or fried dough)

Makes 2 large cups full

Mandlen are crisp small squares that you float in hot soup. They can be bought at grocery shops or supermarkets, but for those of you who like to be absolutely authentic, here is the recipe.

85g (3oz) plain flour and ½ teaspoon salt
1 beaten egg
2 teaspoons vegetable oil

Preheat oven to 180°C (350°F). Sift the flour and salt into a bowl. Make a well in the centre and add the egg and oil. Knead into a soft dough. Divide the dough into two or three pieces, and roll out each piece until thin. Cut the dough into small oblongs about 1cm x 2.5cm (½ inch x 1 inch). Bake for about 20 minutes until golden, or let stand for 30 minutes and fry until golden. Drain off any excess oil, and store them in an airtight container. Add to soup just before serving.

A few weeks before my mother died, it was Yom Kippur. She said that I should learn how to make kreplach. Mother was weak, and had not been out of bed for days.

She came into the kitchen, helped by my sister, and sat across from me at the kitchen bench without her dressing gown, as its weight hurt her shoulders. Her lids were heavy, and her voice faded off after each sentence. I set up the mincer as I had seen her do many times before. It had a shiny barrel and a long handle attached to grind the meat. The pot on the stove bubbled with the boiled meat, and the calf's liver was frying in chicken fat beside it.

Mother instructed me in making the pastry and rolling it out thinly on the bench. When the time came for the kreplach to be assembled, she showed me how to make the three-cornered packages, said to symbolise the three Jewish patriarchs, Abraham, Isaac and Jacob. When the kreplach were bubbling in the broth, and she saw that they did not fall apart, she said her job was now done, and that she could go back to her bed.

kreplach

(meat dumplings)

Makes 40
small dumplings

My father said we should always eat the kreplach, as they were the best part of the soup. Kreplach are Jewish dim sims, just like the ones you could buy at the fish and chip shop that I loved. I ran away from home when I was three years old. I walked for half a kilometre, negotiated a busy street, avoided the trams, and was caught red-handed, sitting up on a stool, ordering two shillings worth of chips. And a dim sim.

The Jews of Russia apparently got the idea for kreplach from the Tartars, who in turn got the concept of pastries with meat (or vegetables) from the Chinese. Jewish dim sims indeed.

Kreplach are made on Kol Nidrei, the eve of Yom Kippur, the Day of Atonement. Kol Nidrei is the evening when orphans say prayers for the souls of their departed parents. Kreplach are eaten in chicken soup, and on the evening of the next day, after the fasting is over, we eat them fried in olive oil, piled on a plate, crispy on the outside, but juicy after the first bite. I can still smell them, while we waited for the first couple to be ready after a long day without food.

Dough:
225g (8oz) plain flour and a pinch of salt
2 eggs, beaten
3–4 teaspoons water
Sieve the flour and salt, make a well in the centre and add the eggs and water.
Mix in the flour until dough is smooth. Set the dough aside and cover with a tea towel.
Let it stand at room temperature while you prepare the filling.

Meat filling:
225g (8oz) gravy beef, boiled
1 large calf's liver, fried in chicken fat (schmaltz)
1 egg, beaten
1 large onion
½ teaspoon salt
black pepper to taste
handful parsley, chopped
3 cloves garlic, crushed
2 tablespoons chicken fat (or schmaltz, available at some delicatessens)

After the beef and liver have been cooked, mince them together finely. Blend all the filling ingredients together, then bind with chicken fat. Flour the bench and roll out dough until it is very thin—the thinnest you can roll without breaking it.
Cut it into 5cm (2 inch) squares, and put a teaspoon of the filling on each.
Fold the square in half, with diagonal corners meeting, to form a triangle.
Wet the edges with water and fold together firmly with your fingers.
Cook the dumplings for about 30 minutes in a large pot of simmering salted water.
Serve in a chicken broth, with a meat meal, or fried for their own sake.

As with other pastry dishes, kreplach can be made with other fillings.
Potato filling: Mash potatoes together with sautéed onions, salt and pepper.
Cheese filling: Cottage cheese mixed with eggs. Season with salt, pepper and sugar.
Kasha filling: Barley, boiled like rice and then mixed with sautéed onions.
Season with salt, pepper and garlic.

Yemenite New Year Soup

Serves 6–8

Jews from Sephardic traditions rather than the Ashkenazi one from whence I came, had many more exotic spices and ingredients to use. Here is a recipe for the equivalent to Eastern European Chicken Broth. Very delicious. It is eaten with flat bread for dipping.

1.5kg (3lbs 6oz) beef shoulder, ribs, or stewing meat (fat removed)
3 veal shanks and 1 large chicken, cleaned and quartered
10–12 cloves garlic, unpeeled
9 small white onions
1 large white turnip, chopped
4 leeks or 8 green onions, coarsely cut
3 celery stalks, chopped
1 medium zucchini (courgette), peeled and cubed
3 carrots, chopped
1 large tomato, quartered
3 potatoes, peeled and diced
1 bunch chopped fresh parsley or fresh coriander (cilantro), woody stems trimmed away
1 tablespoon of a mixture of cumin, coriander (omit if using fresh), curry powder, ginger,
black pepper, and tumeric
salt to taste

Place the beef, veal shanks and chicken in a large pot with enough water to cover them. Bring to the boil, lower the heat, and simmer, until a froth forms. Remove the froth and the chicken from soup. Remove chicken meat from bones. Lower the heat and add the unpeeled garlic cloves (left in their skins, they won't soften in cooking). Add the onion, turnip, and leeks or green onions. Simmer, covered for about 1½ hours or until the meat seems fairly tender. Lift meat out of the soup. Remove all bones and return meat to broth. Cover and simmer another 20 minutes. Let cool and refrigerate overnight. The next day, remove garlic skins if you wish and bring the soup to a boil. Add the celery, zucchini, carrots, tomato and potatoes. Lower the heat, cover, and simmer for 20 minutes. Just before serving, add the parsley or coriander, salt and spices and cook, covered, for a few minutes. Adjust seasonings.

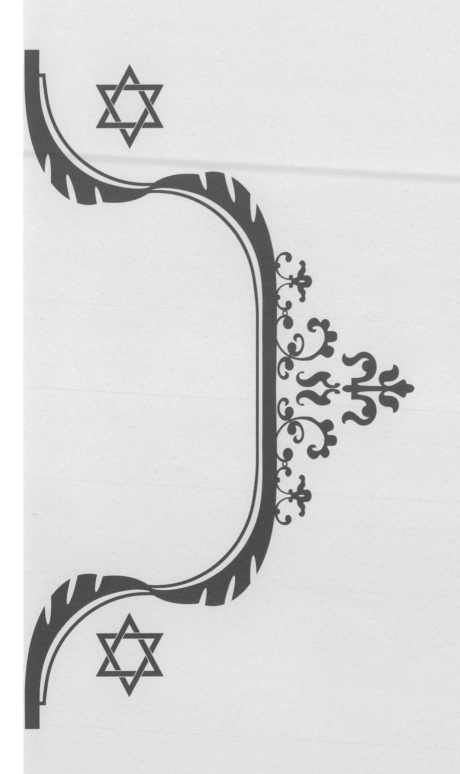

main meals

The main course is generally based on meat or, if there is a dairy product in the meal, fish. Fish is pareve, that is, it is neither milk nor meat, and can be served in a meal that contains either. Fish does not have to be ritually slaughtered like meat. In our home, mother fried fish fillets in hot oil, after they had been dipped in flour and egg. They were crunchy and delicious with her homemade chips.

My mother used to make fish at night and leave it on the side bench, to be eaten the next day. I would wake up and creep out of bed to peer around the kitchen door. If there was no-one there, I would edge to the tray and pick the crunchy bit off the piece on the end.

gawompki
(cabbage rolls)

Makes about 20 rolls

What could be better on a cold, wet night than a plate of steaming cabbage rolls with boiled potatoes and carrots? The cabbage roll is a native dish of Russia and Poland, and there are the usual slight regional differences in presentation and taste. I make them full of meat, but others have been known to mix the filling with rice, and sometimes only to fill them with rice, which I always think is a great disappointment. Cabbage rolls are both sweet and sour, the balance being another regional variation.

The knack to getting these perfect is to select your cabbage properly. The leaves need to be easily peeled away from the body of the cabbage, and that usually means using an oval-shaped cabbage rather than a tall, round one. Oval-shaped with a flat bottom is best. I had never noticed the differences in cabbage shapes before I made cabbage rolls my winter speciality.

My mother taught me how to remove the core of the cabbage and gently pry the cabbage leaves off, making sure they did not break. This sounds easier than it is. Once you have the leaves off, you soften them by putting them into a large vat of boiling water for about 4 or 5 minutes. You then remove them from the water, and pat them dry.

It can be very frustrating getting the cabbage leaves off like this. Once I followed a recipe where the whole of the cabbage head was immersed in boiling water for 5 or 10 minutes, which makes the leaves come off more easily. It worked, but my mother was long dead, so I couldn't tell her about it. She probably would have said that her way was best, and if I wasn't in such a hurry in life, I wouldn't have any trouble with the cabbage leaves.

20 softened cabbage leaves

Filling:
1kg (2lbs 4oz) minced steak
2 onions, chopped
4 eggs
2 cups (110g/4oz) breadcrumbs
salt and pepper to taste
6 cloves garlic, crushed
½ teaspoon sweet paprika
3 tablespoons chopped garden herbs

Mix together all the ingredients until smooth. Place a handful of the mixture in each leaf, fold over one edge and the sides and roll up into a neat, firm package. The outer edge will stay in place once the roll has been lightly fried.

Assembly of the dish:
4 tablespoons olive oil
2 onions, chopped
2 green apples, cored and sliced
2 tablespoons tomato paste or 2 x 400g (14oz) cans of peeled tomatoes, chopped
sugar to taste
1 tablespoon cornflour
juice of 2 lemons
salt and pepper to taste

Using a large enamelled pot, cook the cabbage rolls in hot oil a few at a time, frying them lightly on both sides to keep each roll well sealed. Remove all the rolls from the oil, then fry the onion in the oil. Place a layer of rolls on top of the fried onion. Place a layer of apples, tomato paste or tomatoes, sugar and cornflour on top of rolls, then add another layer of rolls and repeat.
When all the rolls have been assembled in the pot, cover with water, add the lemon juice, salt and pepper, and cook on a low simmer for 2 hours.

schnitzels

Serves 4

Schnitzels were a big favourite in our household until both my children turned vegetarian. Veal or chicken schnitzels were their favourite dish. There were cheers when I announced what was for dinner. Now I go through the same motions using eggplant (aubergine) instead of meat.

4 chicken breasts (or 8 deboned chicken thighs)
or 4 pieces of veal (pounded if you like, but I don't)
flour to coat meat
2 eggs, beaten
salt and black pepper to taste
½ teaspoon paprika
breadcrumbs to coat meat
olive oil

Dip the chicken breasts or veal in flour, then in the eggs, to which you have added pepper, salt and paprika. Roll in breadcrumbs, and fry in very hot oil, with the lid on to retain the juiciness of the meat. Use enough oil to make them float slightly. Make sure the oil is very hot so on first contact the outside of the schnitzel is cooked quickly and doesn't stick to the pan. This takes about 10 minutes each side.

steve polgar is the father of one of my daughter's friends. He was born in Budapest in 1946. He remembers both of his grandmothers cooking for him as a child while his parents went to work.

'Hungarian goulash we know in Australia isn't goulash at all, it's perkelt. If you asked for goulash in Hungary you'd get a completely different dish. Goulash is basically a soup made by people called Gulyas, an ethnic group. They set up a great big basin and throw into it anything that comes to hand. Chopped up animals, vegetables, and then they add potatoes and paprika. Hungarian Jews prefer perkelt.

'My mother prefers a veal goulash—I prefer beef, because I think it has a stronger flavour. It's basically a stew, but the main issue is having it perkelt, that is, singed, if I remember my Hungarian right. I use a Chinese wok, but any sort of pan will do.

'My memory is that there was always plenty of food around. As Hungary has a well-developed agriculture it recovered fairly well after the war, so I can't recall food shortages, although I'm sure there were people who found it difficult. If worst came to worst, you'd make a kind of potato dish like paprika potatoes or something like that, with onions or peppers.

'Both my grandmothers were Jewish but the cooking wasn't kosher at all. My maternal grandmother was quite Orthodox except for the diet. There was no attempt to have a kosher kitchen, except for salting the meat, which was a habit that had remained.

'Apart from that we had ham, and absolutely no attempt was made to separate milk and meat dishes. It was a fairly assimilated Jewish household. In June 1941, when the Germans attacked the Soviet Union, Hungary became the ally of Germany, and this put the Hungarian Jews in a difficult position, as you can imagine. My father converted very early to Catholicism—I think he was only 17—and he remained a Catholic until he died. He was, in fact, a true believer, and he is buried as a Catholic. I went to church and did whatever is appropriate to a Catholic upbringing. Paradoxically, it was taken very seriously in those days because of the Communist opposition to any religion. I don't want to overdo it as terribly radical—it's not as if you had armed thugs waiting for you at the church—it was never like that, but it certainly wasn't the right thing to do if you were hoping to get on in that social structure.

'My father worked for the Hungarian Electricity Commission and was involved in purchasing turbines for new dams and things like that. He found it very anxiety-provoking sort of work. It was seen as bad form to buy the equipment from Western countries, but some of the Eastern manufactured equipment wasn't up to scratch and when things didn't work, it wasn't just a matter of people rebuking you because you were incompetent, it was understood that you were a wrecker of the communist economy. Sometimes people put quite a bit on the line because of the total paranoia of the system at the time. It was just after Stalin died, and it wasn't 'til 1956, when the revolution happened, when the lid was taken off, and people took to the streets.

'My mother is Jewish. It wasn't a problem. We had Passover as well as Christmas. I started my life as a Catholic, and I was about 12 years old when I became a non-Catholic—I became an atheist. When I got married I became "regularised"—do you think this is related to goulash?—I felt Jewish by then, but I had to formalise it and so I was circumcised and I went to the ritual bath, the mikvah.

'For me being Jewish was a gradual thing. I started off as a Catholic, then became an atheist and later, a Jew.'

Hungarian goulash

Serves 6

3 tablespoons olive oil
2 onions, chopped
20g (⅔ oz) sweet Hungarian paprika
1kg (2lbs 4oz) chuck steak; diced, washed in salt water, and drained well
1 tablespoon ground black pepper
1 green capsicum (green pepper), chopped
1 x 400g (14oz) can peeled tomatoes, or 4 tablespoons fresh tomatoes or 1 tablespoon tomato paste
6 cloves garlic, crushed
salt to taste
juice of 1 small lemon
2 good quality stock cubes
1 cup (250ml/8fl oz) water

In a wok or flat pan, heat the oil, and add onions. As they brown, add the paprika, cook for a few minutes, and then perkelt the meat (i.e. brown over at a fairly high flame), stirring the onions in all the time. Add pepper. After stirring, add the green capsicum and then the tomatoes.
Add the garlic, salt, lemon juice, stock cubes and water.
Transfer to a stock pot. Cover and simmer for at least 1–1½ hours. Goulash can be served with rice, mashed potatoes or potato dumplings, and a cucumber salad.

Boiled ox tongue

Serves 6

Boiled ox tongue is the kind of meal you love until you realise what you're eating. Then, if you are a kid you swear never to eat it again. If you are an adult, there are moments when you imagine you are eating your very own tongue, which can put you off your stroke.
Best to serve it already sliced up on a serving plate, for less transparent identification.

1 fresh ox tongue
1 onion, sliced
1 carrot, sliced
6 peppercorns
2 bay leaves
4 cloves

Wash the tongue in cold water for a few minutes. Cover it with cold water in a saucepan
and bring to the boil, removing the scum as it rises. Add vegetables, peppercorns,
bay leaves and cloves. Simmer for 2½–3 hours until tender.
When cooked, pour cold water over the tongue, remove the skin, gristle and any excess fat.
Serve immediately as a hot dish, or serve cold after leaving it overnight in a dish covered
with a plate, and something heavy—a brick or a book—on top to press it down.

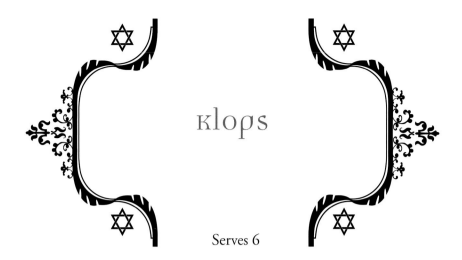

κloρs

Serves 6

Klops is Yiddish for meatloaf. For reasons I can't fathom, the woman who makes a good klops is regarded as being in the sainted class of Jewish mothers. Maybe it's a sign of thrifty housekeeping, as I guess you could get away with a lesser cut of meat if you were clever with the spices. This mixture can be made into smaller balls and individually fried, making them rissoles.

1kg (2lb 4oz) prime minced steak
2 onions, chopped
3 eggs
1½ cups (90g/3oz) breadcrumbs
salt and pepper to taste
½ teaspoon paprika
1 tablespoon parsley, chopped
½ teaspoon nutmeg
1 tablespoon olive oil (optional)

Preheat oven to 210°C (425°F).
Combine ingredients in a blender, then form either one loaf or rissoles.
Roll the loaf or the rissoles in breadcrumbs.
Bake the meatloaf on a baking sheet at 210°C (425°F) until brown and crisp.
If making rissoles, fry them in olive oil, with the lid of the pan on to keep the juices in.

The rules about what you can and cannot do

on the Sabbath are very strict. Because there is to be no work done on this day of rest, the meals have to be thought out well before time.

In Eastern Europe, the life of the kitchen revolved around the wood stove. This was used for cooking, and also for warmth. To start the day's cooking, pails of coals had to be carried from the cellar, while the fire was lit with kindling. Coals were added, and when the fire was stable, vents and dampers were carefully adjusted. After an hour, the stove was at baking temperature. If you lit the stove before night fell on Friday evening, you could cook something slowly overnight and have it ready for the family as they came in from Saturday morning prayers.

Cholent was just such a dish. It is a winter dish, probably from Russia and the Pale of Settlement. The idea is to make a bit of protein go a long way, matched with the need for Orthodox Jews not to cook on the Sabbath. Essentially, this dish consists of a pot with three lamb shanks on the bottom, layers of pulses and potatoes and a potato kugel (pudding) on top to bind the whole thing together. Potato kugel is a separate dish in itself (see recipe on page 78), and not exclusive to a cholent.

Dr Norman Swan is a colleague from the ABC

(Australian Broadcasting Corporation, a paediatrician turned broadcaster and Walkey Award-winning journalist. He was the first Scottish Jew I had ever met, although he assured me there were others.

We were sitting in his kitchen in Balmain, Sydney, over-looking the landscape across a stretch of water, the sun streaming in on my cold Melbourne face.

'One of the prevailing memories of my childhood is waking up on Saturday morning and finding the house filled with the smell of cholent cooking. We never had any central heating and the house was always freezing. Having the oven on all night meant that the kitchen was a lovely warm room to be in. After we ate it for lunch, like all good Jewish families in Glasgow, we'd go to the football in the afternoon!

'My parents were first generation Scottish—my paternal grandparents, the Swirskys, came from Lithuania. My father's mother came from a little shtetl called Dvinsk and to her dying day spoke with a broken accent, while her sister, who was of the same generation, always spoke with a good Scottish accent.'

Glasgow had the third largest Jewish community in Britain after London and Manchester. A lot of working-class Jews lived in the Gorbals, the well-known slum area of Glasgow which almost no longer exists. When Norman was growing up, there were 14 000 Jews in Glasgow, many of them in the rag trade. Norman's maternal grandfather was a credit draper—people bought clothes from him on the 'never never' and he would take his samples and travel, selling to people in their own homes. Then he would visit them each week to get their sixpences to pay off the clothes.

'Many of the Glasgow Jews came to settle there quite by accident. My maternal great-grandfather came in about 1880 or so because Greenoch, on the River Clyde, and indeed Glasgow to a certain extent, was a major port to the United States. People got on the boat at Odessa and bought tickets to New York, but they were conned by the purser and got off at Greenoch. As they couldn't speak English and they didn't know the place from a bar of soap, they thought it was New York.

'What I've never been able to find out is when the moment of revelation came—when they actually discovered that this was not New York, this was in fact Glasgow!

'My great-grandfather David Jacobs did discover quite quickly and was really angry. Two weeks after arriving, he caught the next boat to Newport, Rhode Island, but once he got to America, he hated it and got the next boat back to Glasgow again. You get a story like that from Liverpudlian and Manchester Jews as well, because that's how a lot of them ended up in those places. People who landed in London were generally more intelligent than these others—they went where they were intending to go!'

The cholent is beginning to appear on the bench. Norman's mother or his grandmother would make it using a 'stone' (i.e. 14lb or 6kg) of potatoes. He is trying to cut down the proportions, but this is difficult. I, too, still seem to make great quantities of food by following an old recipe, even though only two or three people may be eating the dish.

'I seem to be making a cholent for 12 people here. I have to admit that I had to phone my mother to confirm the recipe. I told her that she will get full credit as I'll call it "Nannette's Cholent". She was quite thrilled.'

But there was to be a slight disagreement between the Jewish mother and her son the doctor over the matter of soaking the lima beans. Norman explained that his mother is not convinced about health foods. His own family has a high fibre, low fat, low salt diet which is entirely opposite to the Jewish diet. With lima beans and any other pulses, Norman says you are supposed to soak them overnight to get out the alkaloids and other toxins. This also removes the risk of wind, a well-known side effect of cholent. The recipe calls for 500g (1lb 2oz) of lima beans and 500g (1lb 2oz) of split peas. That's a lot of pulses, and the risk of much wind.

'My mother heard my hesitation on the phone and she said "Don't listen to those people who tell you that it's not good to put them straight in. I've been making cholent for years and that's the way to do it, let me tell you." '

Against his mother's advice, Norman soaked the pulses overnight. One of the problems with using dried beans is that you have to keep adding water during the cooking process, as it's very easy for the dish to dry up. Norman thinks that soaking them will avoid this.

'It cooks for 24 hours. You start off high to brown it a little. You put in quite a lot of water and salt and pepper over the layer of potato quarters. When the water boils, you turn it down to medium temperature, probably about 180°C (350°F), and you cook it at medium all afternoon, and then when you go to bed at night you turn it down to the lowest possible light on your oven, having filled it with water for the overnight cooking so that it won't dry out during the night. You top up the water before bed and then in the morning the house is filled with this wonderful smell. I'm having a slight psychological conflict as I make this, delaying putting in the salt and the pepper.'

It appeared that, for Norman, cooking cholent was a dangerous business, especially as he was using an aluminium cooking pot, risking Alzheimer's disease as well.

'You've got to live dangerously if you want to eat Jewish. I'm just putting some olive oil in this pot, but my grandmother would turn in her grave if she thought I was using monounsaturated oil. For anything Jewish you'd have to use chicken fat—schmaltz. Now this has been a very interesting cultural change—it's quite hard to find a Jewish household nowadays where they still use home-made schmaltz.'

Norman describes how schmaltz was made in his family. 'When you make your chicken soup from boiling fowls, you cut off the fat and the skin from the hen and you render them down. The skin becomes crisp and you take it out and use it to make gribenich—you pour salt on the crispy skin, they're the most fantastic things! The rendered down fat makes the chicken schmaltz. And a lot of the taste of Jewish cooking comes from the schmaltz.'

Norman's family, like many others in his neighbourhood, had limited pretensions to orthodoxy, buying kosher meat, but not keeping strictly to the rules of the Sabbath. His father, who ran away from home and a medical course at 18, joined a dance band and played in Big Bands during the war. There were dances to play for on Friday night, so the Sabbath was not observed.

'It's hard to know what his family thought, and whether they were disappointed. It was a very peculiar family, very secretive. There are pictures of my father as a child and he had ringlets, not the ones you see on Orthodox children, but just ringlets—they didn't cut his hair until the age of nine. That must have been fairly scarring in a school in the Gorbals where they'd slit your throat as soon as look at you, and where there was quite a lot of anti-semitism.

'He came back after the war and went into his father's business. As neither my father nor his father were good businessmen, there were a variety of businesses! Originally they were grocers, but then they started a garage in the middle of the Gorbals, in Salisbury Street—Sam Swirsky's Motors. They sold secondhand cars and had a car auction every Wednesday, and they did up cars and garaged people's cars too. Neither my father nor my grandfather were mechanics! They never did well out of it and went bankrupt in a fairly spectacular way when I was about ten. That was a very traumatic period, when my father was basically unemployed for a long time apart from his music. He used to play at the Cameo Ballrooms in Shawlands and he had a Big Band of about twelve people.

'I remember one job he got in that dark period—playing at a Butlins holiday camp. They had to wear red jackets and so on, and as a child I thought this was fantastic because the band was on television. We used to get free passes to go into Butlins for the day and have soggy chips. It was just down the coast from Glasgow and there used to be swimming pools—you can't imagine swimming in Scotland, although where we lived wasn't far from the beach. In summer on a good day we would go to the beach, jump into the water, have a swim, and then come back, get dried, put on a jumper, and have a bowl of cholent!

'As with many other Jewish recipes, cholent has very few herbs and spices. In this Russian version, it is quite plain really, a peasant dish, and this is why the German Jews tend to disdain cooking from the East. They consider themselves higher up the evolutionary scale. If it were Polish, they might put in some sugar, since the Polish Jews liked to sweeten up their main dishes. For example, a Polish lochshen kugel is made with raisins and sugar, but a Russian one is savoury and accompanies the main course.

'So, to make the potato kugel for the top layer, you get a bowl and put in two eggs and four large, finely-grated, peeled potatoes. You have to get the juice out of the potatoes, because there's nothing worse than a soggy kugel. You also need a medium-sized onion, two tablespoons of schmaltz, a level teaspoonful of salt, and about half a cup of self-raising flour. In the end I've actually only used 2–2.5 kilos (4–5lb) of potatoes.

'I'm melting the schmaltz for the kugel and frying the onions, and then combining them with the grated potato, flour, and everything else. The kugel mixture then goes on top of the cholent. A very important thing for any cholent maker to do is to line the bottom of the oven with foil because if it spills over, it makes a hell of a mess.

'When you add the water there should be enough space down the side of the potato kugel to pour the water in. You do this till it reaches the top of the kugel, and then you put the pot back in the oven.'

Norman's mother is the only person he knows in Glasgow who makes cholent and he suspects that it is a dying art.

'There was a Jewish caterer in Glasgow who made cholent but it wasn't as good as my mother's, and my mother's is my grandmother's. I cannot ever remember having cholent anywhere else with this potato kugel on top and so this is unique. It could be a world scoop. If it doesn't work, then it will be because I've soaked the beans against my mother's wishes, so you might just have to cop the alkaloids once a week.'

вaked fish

Serves 4

4 small whole fish or 1 large whole fish in season
(preferably oily fish such as salmon, tuna or snapper)
½ teaspoon salt and black pepper to taste
1 onion, chopped and 1 clove garlic, crushed
1 green capsicum (green pepper), sliced and 2 bay leaves
1 cup (310g/11oz) tomato puree
¼ cup (60ml/2fl oz) oil
1 tablespoon lemon juice
parsley and lemon to garnish

Wash and clean the fish. Sprinkle with salt and black pepper inside. Put onion, garlic,
green capsicum and bay leaves inside the fish. Combine the tomato puree, oil and lemon juice
and pour this over the fish. Wrap the fish in foil, and bake at 180°C (350°F) for 45 minutes.
Remove from foil and discard the bay leaves. Garnish with chopped parsley and lemon.

nannette's cholent with potato kugel

Serves 8

CHOLENT:
2 tablespoons chicken fat (schmaltz), available from some delicatessens
(or substitute with 2 tablespoons olive oil)
3 lamb shanks
500g (1lb 2oz) lima beans
500g (1lb 2oz) yellow split peas
2.5kg (5lbs 10oz) potatoes
salt and pepper to taste
water

Preheat oven to 220°C (450°F). Melt schmaltz in a large pot, layering the lamb shanks along the bottom. Add a layer of lima beans and split peas, and then potatoes which have been cut into quarters or eighths. Sprinkle with salt and pepper, cover with water. Place in oven at 220°C (450°F) for about 10 minutes, then remove and top with kugel layer.

KUGEL:
4 potatoes, peeled, grated and well drained
2 eggs
1 medium-sized onion
2 tablespoons schmaltz (or 2 tablespoons olive oil)
1 teaspoon salt
½ cup (60g/2oz) self-raising flour

Mix all the ingredients together in a bowl. Layer this mixture on top of the cholent, leaving just enough space along the edges of the kugel to pour water into the cholent below. Fill the pot with water up to the top of the kugel and lower oven heat to 180°C (350°F). Cook for about 4–5 hours at this heat, checking occasionally that the dish has not dried out, and topping up water when necessary. Reduce heat to lowest possible setting—about 125°C (240°F)—and cook slowly overnight, making sure the dish is filled with water.

poached fish

Serves 6

Cold poached carp was common as an entrée for the Sabbath meal in Poland. Carp is also cooked in this way by European Jews in Australia, even though carp is considered to be one of the cheaper, less attractive types of fish. The same recipe can be used with Murray perch or even rainbow trout, the fish being cut into steaks rather than fillets.

2–2.5kg (4–5lb) fish steaks
5 cups (1.25 litres/2 pints) water
1 medium onion, sliced and 2 carrots, thinly sliced
10 black peppercorns
2 teaspoons sugar and 1 teaspoon salt

Using a large enamelled pot, bring everything but the fish to the boil, then add the fish steaks. Simmer covered for 1 hour. Cool. Serve fish cold, in the gelatinised liquid, with horseradish.

roast brisket with sauerkraut

Serves 6

This is absolutely the best dish you can have for a main meal. It is one of the only things that makes waiting for dessert worthwhile. The combination of slightly fatty meat, with plenty of bones for gnawing means you can satisfy many carnivorous yearnings at once—the hunger for a full belly, for marrow from soft bones and for the firmness of white cartilage between strong teeth.

I am not a vegetarian. With dietary rules, the important thing, I think, is to know and be mindful of what we do. I don't eat meat from mistreated animals, which means most commercial poultry is off the menu. But I have seen noble hunters bring kangaroo back to camp, and distribute it in solemn and holy fashion to their friends and family.

1kg (2lbs 4oz) double brisket or short ribs of beef
4 cloves garlic, crushed
salt and pepper to taste
1 teaspoon cinnamon
1 tablespoon olive oil
6 large tomatoes, skinned or peeled, or 2 tablespoons tomato paste
3 large onions, sliced
500g (1lb 2oz) sauerkraut (I prefer vacuum packed to tinned)
6 tablespoons sugar

Preheat oven to 125°C (240°F).
Rinse the meat in cold salty water and dry it.
Rub meat with garlic and sprinkle with salt, pepper and cinnamon.
Heat the oil in a large flameproof dish and brown the meat on all sides.
Add the tomatoes and onions, cover the dish, transfer to the oven and cook very slowly at
125°C (240°F) for 4 hours, or until the meat is tender.
Half an hour before the meal is ready, drain the sauerkraut and cover it with water in a saucepan.
Bring to the boil, add the sugar and some of the tomato and onion from the meat.
Cover and cook for 20 minutes.
Serve sauerkraut hot with the delicious meat.

ROAST DUCK

Serves 4

'On special occasions,' my mother would say, 'we would have roast chicken together with a piece of veal, roast brisket, and a beautiful roast duck from the yard. Something for everyone!'
So what is simpler than roasting a bird? 'The secret,' she whispered, 'is in the basting'.

1 duck (approx. 2kg/4lbs 8oz)
1 medium-sized onion, sliced
1 medium-sized carrot, roughly chopped
handful of parsley
salt and pepper to taste
1 tablespoon brown sugar
1 teaspoon salt
⅓ cup (80ml/3fl oz) hot water

Preheat oven to 180°C (350°F). Dry the duck inside and out after washing in cold salty water. Place onion, carrot, parsley, salt and pepper inside the bird. Dissolve the sugar and
1 teaspoon of salt in the hot water and use to glaze the outside of the duck.
Cook for 30 minutes at 180°C (350°F). Remove the duck from the baking dish.
Prick its skin and drain off and discard the fat which flows out. Return the duck to the
baking dish and cook for a further 1–1½ hours. Baste with pan juices every 20 minutes.

VARIATION: ROAST VEAL WITH CHICKEN

Prepare the chicken as for the duck above, but instead of glazing with salt,
sugar and water, rub its entire body with salt, pepper and 2–3 cloves of crushed garlic.
Prepare a leg of veal in the same way, and bake both together for 1½ hours at 180°C (350°F).
When both are almost cooked, put 2 cups of cooked pasta around the meat to soak up the pan juices.
Cook for a further 15 minutes then serve with salad or vegetables and the pasta.

tsimmes fleisch

Serves 6

Tsimmes is the yiddish word for a sweet carrot dish. It is usually served as a vegetable accompaniment for the main meal, but here the carrots are combined with beets, turnips and meat to make a main meal.

3 teaspoons salt and ½ teaspoon pepper
1.5kg (3lb 6oz) brisket of beef
2 onions, chopped
2 tablespoons flour
3 cups (750ml/1 pint 6fl oz) boiling water
¼ cup (60ml/2fl oz) honey or to taste
8 carrots, coarsely grated
1 turnip, coarsely grated
1 beetroot, coarsely grated
1 sweet potato, peeled and quartered (optional)

Preheat oven to 180°C (350°F).
Mix 2 teaspoons of the salt and the ½ teaspoon of pepper, and rub it into the beef.
Place in a heavy pot with the onions and brown slowly over a medium heat. Add the flour, mixing well.
Then add the water, stirring, until it reaches boiling point. Cover and simmer slowly for about 1 hour.
Pour the honey in with the meat, then add the vegetables and remaining salt.
Cover and bake at 180°C (350°F) for 1½ hours, removing the cover for
the last 15–20 minutes to brown the surface.

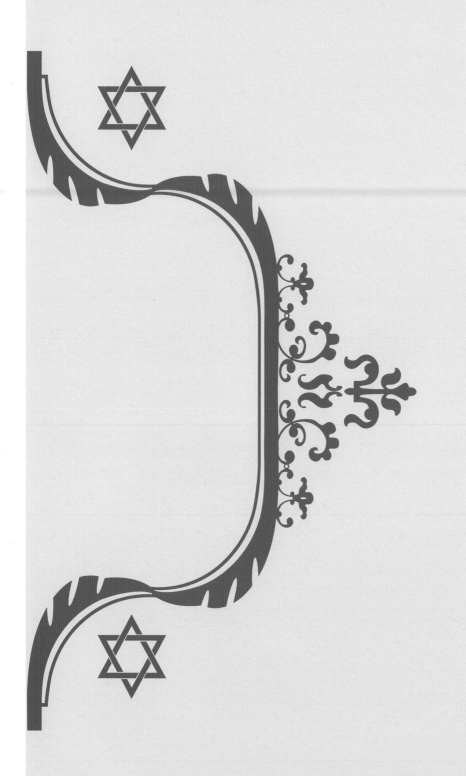

vegetables

Vegetables suffered at our house. We wanted the local ethnic tucker—chops, 'snags', hamburgers, roast lamb and gravy. We spent our days in the street playing with the Catholic family from across the road and when it was dinner time, we could see the preparations and smell the roasts, the 'three veg' and the gravy. We wanted peas and mint sauce, and still more gravy, and so our table changed to reflect the tastes of working-class Australia. Mum and Dad didn't mind because it fitted in with their concern for us not to speak with a foreign accent. Away with Yiddish, Hebrew, Polish, Russian, French and other tongues—on with English! In the end we would be complimented for having had elocution lessons. But it may well have been the mint sauce.

aaron Rynie's Latkes
(potato pancakes)

Serves 4

My father rarely cooked. When my mother went to hospital to have my sister, Dad and I lived on fish and chips for a week. He would sometimes fry up Polish sausage and onions for lunch on Saturdays, and once a year he would make us latkes. Traditionally they are eaten during Channukah, the Festival of Lights, but in our home food could stand on its own, without ceremony. When the crisp, brown pancakes were drained of their oil, we sprinkled them with sugar. The edges were a filigree of sweet crunchiness.

6 potatoes, grated
1 large onion, chopped
2 cloves garlic
1 egg
30g (1oz) plain flour
salt and pepper to taste
olive oil for frying

Combine the potatoes and onions, add the remaining ingredients and mix into a batter.
Heat oil in a pan, and when very hot, drop in about 2 dessertspoons of batter for each latke.
Fry the latkes on each side until they are crisp and brown. There are other variations on latkes, including the one following which adds other vegetables and cheese to the mix.

variation: zucchini parmesan Latkes

To the basic latke mixture above add:
1kg (2lb 4oz) zucchini (courgettes), grated
½ tablespoon lemon juice
½ cup (60g/2oz) grated parmesan cheese
half bunch parsley, chopped
2 teaspoons sugar

Method as above.

potatoes with sour cream

Serves 4–6

We like potatoes so much we even have a song about them called 'Zuntig Bulbes' which refers to eating potatoes every day except for the Sabbath, when you eat Potato Kugel as a treat.

1kg (2lb 4oz) potatoes, peeled
½ small onion, finely chopped
¾ cup (190ml/7fl oz) sour cream
salt and pepper to taste
30g (1oz) butter
chopped parsley for garnish

Preheat oven to 200°C (400°F). Boil the potatoes whole in salty water until they are just tender. Drain and slice then layer them with the onion in a greased dish. Combine the sour cream with salt and pepper, and pour this over the potatoes. Cut the butter into small pieces and dot over the surface. Bake for about 20 minutes until the top is golden brown.

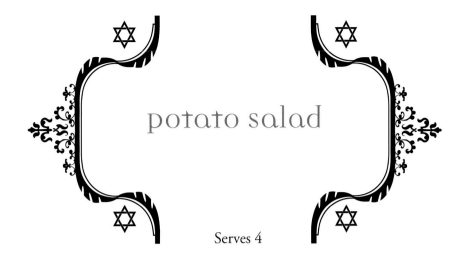

potato salad

Serves 4

As you can see, in a poor Eastern European shtetl, the more creative you can be with potatoes, the better.

1kg (2lb 4oz) waxy new potatoes, whole
4 tablespoons olive oil and 2 tablespoons balsamic vinegar
salt and coarsely ground black pepper, to taste
4 cloves garlic, crushed
3 hard-boiled eggs, chopped
3 pickled dill cucumbers, chopped
4 spring onions, finely chopped and a handful chopped parsley

Boil the potatoes in salted water until soft (but not floury). Cool, then peel and chop into cubes.
Combine oil, balsamic vinegar, salt, pepper and garlic in a bowl to make a vinaigrette.
Pour over potatoes, then fold in eggs, cucumbers, onions and parsley.

tsimmes
(sweet carrots)

Serves 4

This dish is, in its simplest form, carrots glazed with sugar or honey. But even more delicious is this recipe, which allows the addition of sultanas and ginger.

3 tablespoons (about 90g/3oz) chicken fat (schmaltz) or butter
4 large carrots, peeled and sliced
½ cup (90g/3oz) brown sugar
1½ cups (375ml/12fl oz) water
¼ teaspoon salt
½ teaspoon ginger
½ cup (90g/3oz) sultanas

Melt the fat or butter in a pan and add the carrots, cooking them until they are browned lightly. Boil the sugar and water together for 5 minutes, and then add to the carrots. Cook gently, covered, until the carrots are tender. Stir in salt, ginger and sultanas, and serve hot.
Serves 4

eggplant kugel

Serves 4

A kugel is a pudding, and it can be savoury as in the one below, or sweet, as you will find later in this book. Either way, a kugel is a signal of hearth and heart—a simple homely dish.

1 large eggplant (aubergine)
1 onion, chopped
2 cloves garlic, crushed
1 green capsicum (green pepper), chopped
60g (2oz) butter
2 eggs, lightly beaten
salt and pepper to taste
1 cup (60g/2oz) breadcrumbs or matzo meal
½ cup (125ml/4fl oz) melted butter, extra
about ½ teaspoon paprika

Preheat oven to 200°C (400°F).
Peel and slice the eggplant and cook in simmering salt water until it is tender.
Drain it to rinse off any bitterness, then mash it.
Sauté the onion, garlic and green capsicum in butter until tender.
Mix the eggplant with the eggs, add salt and pepper to taste.
Add the onion, garlic and capsicum to the eggplant mixture, blend in the breadcrumbs
or matzo meal, and place in a greased casserole dish. Pour melted butter over the kugel, sprinkle
it with paprika and bake for 45 minutes at 200°C (400°F) until the top is brown and the sides are crusty.

stuffed eggplant

Serves 4

A perfectly respectable (and delicious) vegetarian dish, and yet another way to cook an eggplant.

4 eggplants (aubergines)
2 red capsicums (red peppers)
60g (2oz) butter
2 small onions, chopped
½ cup (60g/2oz) grated cheese
1 cup (60g/2oz) breadcrumbs
salt and pepper to taste

Preheat oven to 200°C (400°F).
Cook the eggplants in boiling salt water for 15 minutes, removing the stalks first.
Drain, then put them in a dish of cold water until they are cool enough to handle.
Chop one and a half capsicums and slice the remaining half capsicum into lengthwise strips.
Melt the butter in a saucepan and cook the onions and the chopped red capsicum gently
for 5 minutes. Add the cheese, breadcrumbs, and salt and pepper.
Halve the cooked eggplants, scoop out and mash the flesh, then add it to the
red capsicum and onion mixture. Fill the eggplant cases with this mixture,
place on a greaseproof dish or tray, and bake at 200°C (400°F) for 30 minutes.
Garnish with slices of the leftover capsicum 5 minutes before the stuffed eggplants are ready.

pumpkin was for horses, my mother said. In Poland, people didn't eat it. As a girl, she had a horse with one ear, who loved pumpkin. After the war, when she travelled back to her village of Wyrozeby there was no sign of her family, and her home had been destroyed, but she saw the horse being ridden through the streets by a neighbour.

'Hey, that's my horse,' she said.

'You want it back?' said the neighbour.

She rode it again, but she was headed for Paris and thought a horse with one ear might be out of place. So she kissed it and left it in the fields eating pumpkin. We had to eat pumpkin because it might save our lives—we would be able to run fast and survive, like the horse with one ear.

I had my own formative experience with pumpkin at kindergarten. Everyone has a Cinderella story.

One day, I led a swarm of children around the garden at play lunch, and we picked the youngest, most perfect flowers, buds and leaves from the plants. We were like locusts, stripping every shrub, uprooting irises and lilies and the 'mirror' bushes. I said that if we planted them in the sandpit, vegetables would grow.

Our teacher, Miss Sampson, was not pleased. She asked why there were so many ruined plants in the sandpit, and they told her what I had said.

The next day, a Greek boy called George was digging in the pit, and came across something with a hard orange surface.

'Hey,' he said, 'what's this?' I peered at it as we dug and dug, and as I recognised the shape, my eyes widened.

A pumpkin. A large, round, green and orange pumpkin.

'See Ramona,' said Miss Sampson, 'just as you said. A pumpkin has grown there overnight.'

I was mystified, but quick enough to take the credit. 'I told you so,' I said. But I watched Miss Sampson carefully afterwards. Too young to be appreciative, I thought her dark eyes could see right into my soul.

cucumber salad

Serves 4

A creamy, savoury dish, best served chilled—perfect with Hungarian Goulash (see recipe page 68).

1 cucumber, peeled and diced
2 tomatoes, diced
6 spring onions, chopped
1 cup (250ml/8fl oz) sour cream
500g (1lb 2oz) cottage cheese
salt and black pepper to taste

Combine all ingredients just before serving.

vegetables didn't count for much at our place.

We waited for the meat, which was in its turn a mere stop on the way to the true destination—dessert. Correction. The desserts we had were stewed fruit, with plenty of great, sweet, slimy prunes, which we had to eat for our regularity. The dessert was really a path to the cakes. And the lemon tea. And more cakes.

The vegetables tended to be boiled to the point of surrender. Roughage was not an issue—for our health and good temper, my mother gave us cod liver oil. (I can still remember the retching that used to come upon me as she unscrewed the top of the evil dark-brown bottle.)

I'm not saying that she didn't try with vegetables. But the war had made both my parents into carnivores. A meal was not a meal for my father unless there was red meat, and sometimes chicken as well, and roast brisket. Years of hunger had created a desperation about food. There was a drive to display, to show that there was plenty today and would be plenty tomorrow.

My father told us how during the war he would sneak out at night from the cellar where he spent 3 years hiding, to gather rotten potatoes from the fields. They would use every bit of the vegetable, with the peel used for soup or for making vodka. He used to eat onions raw, even after the war, after the move through Paris, to the cosmopolitan Australian slum of St Kilda and on to the very Anglo suburb of North Balwyn. It was as if meat could banish those memories for him.

desserts

Dessert is simply a slight detour on the way to the main event—cake with tea or coffee. Often it is stewed fruit compote (kompot in Yiddish) featuring apples and raisins, plums or, for medicinal purposes, prunes. Jews are overly fond of prunes for their promotion of regularity. Enough said on this matter in a book of cooking. Sometimes blintzes are served as a more substantial dessert when the meal has contained no meat, as a milchich (milk/dairy) meal will usually be lighter than a fleishig (meat) one.

Baked Apples

Serves 4

Not another apple recipe? Imagine what it would have been like to live in Poland and have nothing but apples to cook with. Stop complaining. These are delicious!

4 Granny Smith apples
4 tablespoons (90g/3oz) butter
4 tablespoons (90g/3oz) mixed dried fruits
4 tablespoons brandy
3 teaspoons sugar and 2 teaspoons cinnamon

Preheat oven to 180°C (350°F). Wash and core the apples.
Mix butter, dried fruit, brandy and cinnamon together. Fill the centre of each apple with this mixture. Bake in 3cm (1 inch) of water in a shallow dish for about 50 minutes.
Sprinkle with sugar and cinnamon and serve with cream.

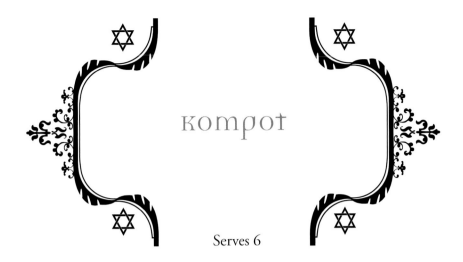

Kompot

Serves 6

Kompot is Yiddish for compote of fruit, which is an easy and simple way to use a combination of fresh and dried fruits. Use rosewater instead of vanilla essence for a more Sephardic flavour.

6 apples, peeled and sliced
½ cup (90g/3oz) raisins or sultanas
1 cup (140g/5oz) dried apricots or peaches, or both
1 teaspoon vanilla essence
2 tablespoons sugar
½ cup (170g/6oz) pine nuts or blanched almonds
water to almost cover the fruit

Heat all the ingredients over a low flame for about 15 minutes until the fruit is soft.
Cool. Serve with ice-cream or cream or on its own.

YANKA ENKER IS THE MOTHER OF DEBI ENKER, the television critic I've interviewed on my radio programs. She is softly beautiful, her blond and grey hair piled up on her head, a more Polish than Jewish beauty. This is how she survived the war in Europe, by taking the identity of a Christian and living undercover. I wondered if in Poland she had ever walked by my own mother—perhaps they had a conversation in perfect Polish or perfect German, without a hint of a Jewish accent.

Debi and her husband, Tom Ryan, a good Irishman, swore that Yanka's cheese blintzes were worth dying for. Here Yanka explains how to do it.

'The flour should be sifted and not lumpy. This is much easier now than years ago, because now I have electrical appliances, but I used to do it by hand.

'I am from Krynica, which was a beautiful holiday resort in Poland. We had a guesthouse on a hill, in the mountains. I had a very beautiful childhood because I spent lots of time in the fresh air and I saw people all the time. My parents worked very, very hard—it is a demanding job, running a guesthouse. Jewish people would stay there, it was kosher, and my parents were very Orthodox.

'My mother didn't cook, but she supervised the cook. I learned this recipe for blintzes from my cousin Fela, and from my friend Genia here. Genia's a terrific cook but she's modest.

'When we lived in Rumania, we had a little flat and I would cook in the bathroom for my husband and his brother. I was experimenting on them, really, I didn't have a clue how to cook. I look back, and I think, my goodness, how did they manage to eat? But I learned, slowly, from my cousin Fela when we lived together.

'I used to make blintzes with potatoes—russkiye piroshki—I use the dry ones because the other kinds turn watery and blackish and the colour isn't nice. You have to get the frying pan hot—that is the secret of blintzes.

'Cooking was different in Poland. It was simple. And if simple food is prepared in a tasty way, I prefer it. In some restaurants, the names are very elaborate but they are really simple dishes underneath. The majority of Jews in Poland were poor, so they didn't use a lot of expensive ingredients. Even chicken was expensive: poultry was only for Friday night or for holidays. You added eggs and matzo meal to fish to make it go further, and that's gefillte fish—now, nobody does it because it's cheaper, but because they like the taste.

'I also used to make the cheese—you let the milk stand with a little bit of sour cream in it for a few days, and it goes like yoghurt. Then we would place it in a cloth bag in the shape of the cheese, and put something heavy on it like a brick. Austrians do the same, Germans do the same—the blintz is very common in that part of Europe.'

cheese blintzes

Makes 12

Batter:
3 eggs
1 cup (170g/6oz) plain flour, sifted
1 cup (250ml/8fl oz) milk
butter for frying

Beat eggs until light and fluffy, add sifted flour and beat again. Add milk and stir. Leave to stand for 10 minutes so that the batter will thicken. Melt 1 teaspoon of butter in a frying pan until hot, and add enough batter to cover the bottom of the pan. Fry on one side, then the other, then set aside. Repeat, melting a fresh teaspoon of butter in the pan for each new pancake.

Filling:
500g (1lb 2oz) cottage cheese
1 egg
½ cup (90g/3oz) sultanas
½ cup (140g/5oz) sugar
2 teaspoons grated orange rind

Combine cheese, egg, sultanas, sugar and orange rind.
Place 2 flat tablespoons of filling in the centre of each pancake. Fold in at opposite sides then wrap up into parcels, quickly fry again. Serve warm with vanilla sugar sprinkled on top, and sour cream as well.

Alternative savoury filling
For savoury blintzes, called piroshki after the Russian recipe, combine about 500g (1lb 2oz) of mashed potato, 1 onion (chopped and fried), a handful of dried mushrooms and salt and pepper to taste. Fill as above.

crunchy nut kugel

Serves 4

This kugel is similar to the Lochshen Kugel, but this variation has a delicious, nutty toffee flavour.

200g (7oz) salted butter or margarine, melted
¾ cup (140g/5oz) dark brown sugar
1 cup (140g/5oz) walnuts or almonds, halved
500g (1lb 2oz) pasta or egg noodles, cooked
4 large eggs
1 teaspoon cinnamon
½ cup (140g/5oz) sugar
2 teaspoons salt

Preheat oven to 180°C (350°F). Coat a deep baking dish with about ¼ cup of melted butter. Press the brown sugar into the bottom and press the nuts into the sugar. Mix cooked noodles with the eggs, remaining melted butter, cinnamon, sugar, and salt and pour into the pan.
Bake at for 1 hour and 15 minutes or until the top is brown.
Let sit for 15 minutes before turning out. The top will be slightly hard like toffee.
Serve cold or at room temperature.

lochshen kugel

Serves 4

This is a traditional, sweet, baked pudding, not unlike the idea of an English bread and butter pudding. You can use macaroni, flat pasta or various egg noodles. If, like me, you regularly find yourself with left over pasta because judging pasta quantities is so difficult, this is a great way to use it up.

1 x 500g (1lb 2oz) packet pasta or egg noodles, cooked
500g (1lb 2oz) cottage cheese
½ cup (90g/3oz) sultanas
handful of dried apricots, diced
½ cup (140g/5oz) sugar or jam
handful of prunes, seeded and chopped
handful of walnuts, roughly chopped
2 eggs

Preheat oven to 180°C (350°F).
Combine the ingredients, and put in a buttered baking dish. Cover with foil.
Bake for 1 hour and serve hot.

variation: apple kugel

Replace the prunes and dried apricots with 4 peeled and sliced
Granny Smith apples, the juice of 1 lemon and 3 tablespoons of brandy.

Baked Apple Rice Kugel

Serves 4

Rice quantities can also be hard to judge. Thank goodness you can also make this kugel which uses leftover rice instead of pasta. You can also replace the apples with berries in season or raisins.

¾ cup (225g/8oz) arborio rice
3¼ cups (800ml/1¼ pints) milk
140g (5oz) sugar
½ teaspoon nutmeg
salt to taste
1 teaspoon vanilla essence
½ teaspoon cinnamon
3 egg yolks
4 large Granny Smith apples (sliced)

Preheat oven to 180°C (350°F). Parboil and drain rice, then add it to the milk. Bring to the boil, then simmer on low heat for 25 minutes. Add sugar, nutmeg, salt, vanilla and cinnamon. Beat in yolks and stir on a low flame until the consistency of custard. Layer the mixture alternating with apple slices in an oven dish. Bake at 180°C (350°F) for 20 minutes.

quinces in syrup

Serves 6

The quince always seems an unfriendly fruit as you can't simply pick them off a tree and eat them. They must be persuaded—which this recipe does beautifully. Italian Jews serve poached quinces in a clove-and-cinnamon-scented syrup at Rosh Hashanah, the Jewish New Year celebration, and to break the fast at Yom Kippur.

1kg (2lb 4oz) quinces

Syrup:
2 cups (500g/1lb 2oz) sugar
1 cup (250ml/8fl oz) water, or as needed
1 tablespoon chopped fresh rosemary
2 whole cloves
2 cinnamon sticks

In a large saucepan, combine the quinces, whole and unpeeled, with water to cover.
Bring to the boil over high heat and cook, uncovered, until just tender (about 30–40 minutes).
Drain the quinces and, when cool enough to handle, peel, halve, core, and cut into slices.
In a saucepan large enough to accommodate the sliced quinces, combine
the sugar, water, rosemary, cloves, and cinnamon sticks.
Place over medium heat and bring to a simmer, stirring to dissolve the sugar.
Add the quinces and additional water if needed to cover. Simmer for 5 minutes.
Then bring the quince slices to a boil in the syrup three times, boiling them for 5 minutes
each time. This helps to bring up the rich red color of the fruit and allows them to absorb
the syrup over time. The length of time over which the boiling happens determines
the redness of the quinces. Transfer to a serving dish and refrigerate.
Serve chilled.

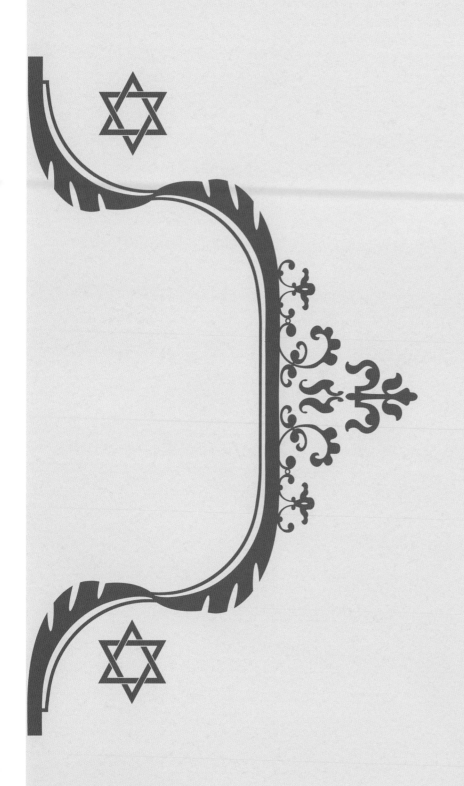

cakes

The Monarch Cake Shop is in Acland Street, St Kilda. Its shelves groan with cakes laden with layers of mocha and strawberries, and chocolate on chocolate. Is this a sane way to display food—shelf upon shelf of trays of intricate sugar and flour combinations? My eyes skim the florentines, the chocolate kugelhopf, and always come to rest on the poppyseed cake.

poppyseed cake

I first remember having poppyseed cake at afternoon teas with elderly ladies my mother had befriended. Tea in delicate china cups, the milk poured in first, and served with a slice of poppyseed cake, filled with raisins. Sometimes I thought I could taste a little alcohol too, but maybe that was just the richness and the blackness of the poppy seeds.

My sister and I had to be very good on these visits, and sometimes we were allowed to play our hostess' piano too. It smelt of wood and polish, and was invariably covered with a lace doily.

One of the ladies was Mrs Kaminski, the woman who made custom fitted brassieres. My mother went to her for fittings, and Mrs Kaminski had dressmaker's models of all shapes and sizes in her bedroom. The garments were hand-stitched, and made of pink satin. They were very beautiful, and I understood that these were intimate matters for which my mother had to undress behind the bedroom screen. It was like going to the doctor's, except that they didn't have poppyseed cake at the doctor's.

Mrs Kaminski had a son, an only son, who sometimes played with us. As I grew older I remember feeling sorry and embarrassed for him, that his mother had this brassiere business going, and that he had to have troops of ladies doing intimate things in his mother's bedroom, a room that smelled of perspiration and perfume. It turned from a doctor's surgery to a house of ill-repute in my mind's eye. Later I heard that he had broken his mother's heart by finding old-time religion and refusing to eat with her because she was not keeping a kosher home.

'This is why she suffered in a camp,' said my mother with a sigh, 'so that her son should tell her she isn't kosher enough?'

Filling:
1 cup (255g/9oz) sugar and 1 cup (250ml/8fl oz) milk
255g (9oz) ground poppy seeds
⅓ cup (60g/2oz) raisins and ⅓ cup (60g/2oz) glace orange peel, diced
1 tablespoon grated lemon rind
2 large egg whites, lightly beaten
30g (1oz) softened unsalted butter

In a saucepan, combine the sugar and the milk, and bring to the boil. Add the poppy seeds, raisins, orange peel and lemon rind. Mix well. Cool, then add the egg whites and butter.

Pastry:
1 tablespoon active dry yeast
1⅓ cups (310ml/11fl oz) milk
¾ cup (200g/7oz) sugar and 4 cups (700g/1lb 9oz) plain flour
60g (2oz) unsalted butter
1 large egg

In a small bowl, combine the yeast, ⅓ cup of warm milk and 1 teaspoon each of sugar and flour. After about 15 minutes it should be foamy. Bring 1 cup of milk to the boil and remove from heat. Stir in the sugar and butter. Cool. Combine the milk mixture with 2 cups of the plain flour, the egg and the yeast mixture. Beat until smooth. Gradually add the rest of the flour, and beat until the dough is smooth. Knead it on a floured board. It should still be a little sticky. Put the dough in a buttered bowl, turning it over to coat the whole surface with butter and cover it with a tea towel. Let it stand to rise in a warm place for 1–1½ hours. It should double in volume. Preheat oven to 180°C (350°F). Punch the dough down, roll it into a rectangle measuring 60 x 30cm (24 x 12 inches) and spread the poppy seed filling over it to 2.5cm (1 inch) from the edges. Roll it up, beginning with the long side and folding in the short sides, and place it seam downwards on a buttered baking sheet. Let it rise again, in a warm place for an hour.
Brush the top with water or milk, or a beaten egg, and bake at 180°C (350°F) for 45 minutes.

Glaze:
When it has cooled, glaze the cake by mixing together 2 cups (400g/14oz) of icing sugar with 2 tablespoons of lemon juice and 2 tablespoons of boiling water. Beat together until light and fluffy. Spread it on the cake, and let it stand until the glaze is set.

emma's honey cake

This cake, the favourite of my elder daughter, is meant to symbolise a good and sweet year, and is served especially at Rosh Hashanah, the New Year's celebration. Come to think of it, Emma cooks it often when she entertains. And why not have a good and sweet New Year all year round? The cake may not help, but it can't hurt.

3 eggs
1 cup (250ml/8fl oz) honey
1 cup (255g/9oz) sugar
1 cup (250ml/8fl oz) warm black coffee
½ cup (125ml/4fl oz) olive oil
2¾ cups (450g/1lb) self-raising flour
2 teaspoons vanilla essence
½ teaspoon allspice

Optional:
1 teaspoon cinnamon
1 teaspoon ginger
1 teaspoon ground cloves
2 teaspoons whisky
half a handful slivered almonds or walnuts
half a handful raisins.

Preheat oven to 180°C (350°F).
Beat the eggs with the honey and sugar. Add the coffee and then the oil,
beat again for a few minutes, then add the rest of the ingredients.
Bake in a round ring tin for 1 hour.

dark chocolate cake

This cake is a breeze because it's not at all fiddly. I guarantee that (almost) anyone can make it.

Cake:
2 cups (340g/12oz) plain flour
1 teaspoon baking soda
1¼ cups (310g/11oz) sugar
½ cup (60g/2oz) cocoa
pinch salt
2 teaspoons vanilla essence
1¼ cups (310ml/10fl oz) milk
60g (2oz) butter or margarine
3 whole eggs and 1 egg yolk
1 cup (110g/4oz) shredded coconut

Preheat oven to 180°C (350°F). Mix together all dry ingredients except the coconut, and
gradually add in all the others. Place half of the batter into a greased pan.
Add the coconut in an even layer.
Cover coconut with remaining batter. Bake for 55–60 minutes.

Filling:
1 egg white
¼ cup (60g/2oz) sugar
1 cup (110g/4oz) shredded coconut
1 teaspoon vanilla
1 tablespoon plain flour

Beat the egg white and gradually add the sugar until the mixture is stiff, then add the other ingredients. When the cake is cool, cut it in half and spread the filling between the halves. If you wish you can make a rich chocolate frosting to go over the top—this really is going over the top though, as the cake alone is very rich. This is worth at least 2 aerobics classes or 100 laps of a 25-metre swimming pool.

Frosting:
200g (7oz) cooking chocolate
60g (2oz) butter or margarine
½ cup (125ml/4fl oz) milk
1 egg yolk
2½ cups (450g/1lb) icing sugar

Melt the chocolate and butter in a saucepan over a low heat. Add milk. Cool mixture, then beat in egg yolk. Add sugar slowly, beating with a fork all the time. Spread over the cake.

professor peter singer has a world reputation as a philosopher in ethics. The author of the famous and influential book Animal Liberation, Peter was born of Austrian parents who came to Australia just before the outbreak of the Second World War. He is married to Renate, who was born in Poland and emigrated with her parents in 1952.

Marion, the middle daughter of three is in the process of moving out to live with some friends for the summer, that magical time between the end of the school year and the beginning of tertiary studies. She has delayed her exit, however, until the ponchkes are ready.

Ponchkes are Jewish jam doughnuts. They are a traditional food made for Channukah, the Festival of Lights, which celebrates the miracle of the oil that was meant to last in the lamp for one day, but lasted for eight. Foods cooked in oil are traditionally eaten as one reads about the victory of Judah and the Maccabees.

Renate explains the origins of ponchkes in their household. 'This friend of mine had children late in life. She's married to a non-Jewish person and she suddenly decided her children should experience some of the traditions that she'd never even had herself, so we started having Channukah at the beach together. It's not actually a very traditional Channukah because it's in January for a start. But we go to her place, and she makes latkes and Peter makes ponchkes.'

Peter has already made the dough, and placed it in a warm place by the sunny window to prove.

'What went into this is 2½–3 cups of plain flour and then some milk. That brings us to the first problem, if you want to make sure of the ethics involved. To provide milk, cows have to be repeatedly made pregnant, and their calves have to be taken away from them so that we can always have milk. Since cows, like us, are mammals and have a strong attachment to their calves, it causes them pain. So, if you don't have to use milk, why use it? Soy milk is very widely available now and it's perfectly nutritious, so it does very well.

'So we use ¾ cup (190ml/7fl oz) of soy milk, a couple of tablespoons of sugar in the soy milk, and then some yeast—I used two sachets of dry yeast and then mixed the warmed milk, sugar and yeast together. You wait till it sort of froths up nicely, about 10 minutes. The flour has a pinch of salt added into it, as well as a couple of egg yolks, and this is where you come upon another ethical problem.

'I use free range eggs because I wouldn't use any others. Most of the eggs that people buy in supermarkets come from hens that are kept in cages. About four hens to a cage, hardly bigger than the size of this board, really. They're incredibly crowded, and they can't stretch their wings or walk around in the normal way, they can't do any of the things that hens normally do, like scratch around in the dirt. They're so distressed that they peck each other and then their beaks have to be cut back to stop them from killing each other. It's one of the worst forms of animal abuse.

'When we have the warm milk with the sugar in it, all nice and frothy from the yeast, we pour it into the flour, salt and egg yolks, and mix it up into a dough. Then we work about a tablespoonful of margarine into the dough plus a pinch of cinnamon for flavour. Actually, the soy milk that I use is vanilla soy milk, which gives the whole thing a vanilla flavour.

'This dough is basically like a bread dough, but slightly richer, and it produces a softer sort of doughnut than if you used bread dough.

After the dough has been rising for 2 hours, Peter rolls it out flat to about 1cm thick.

'I don't really remember my father cooking at all. You see, neither of my parents cooked very much, because we always had someone at home to help with that sort of thing. My mother, being a doctor, was at work as well and so they would cook at weekends or on special occasions, but not a great deal. My grandmother lived with us until I was about 10, when she died, and she would cook pastry-like things, not this sort of stuff. When she cooked apple strudel, she would roll the pastry out very, very thinly, which was a lot of work. My aunt's family were a little more interested in Jewish things than we were—my cousin had a Bar Mitzvah. I told him he was only doing it for the presents.

Peter is making the doughnuts by pulling off walnut-sized bits of the dough and forming them roundly with his hands. He also cuts alternative shapes from the rolled out dough with an upside-down glass.

'Now Ramona's made me think more seriously about how to put the jam in—it's actually not jam, it's povidl, a concentrate of plums. Should we put it in before or after we fry the dough in oil? It's for posterity now, you see.

We decided that the way to do it was to insert a small spoonful of povidl into the pastry, and then pull the pastry over the hole, and lower the doughnut into the hot oil. We all remembered buying fresh doughnuts with hot jam, and figured that the jam must have been through the frying process too.

'As Renate said, this is not a very old tradition in our family because we were never very big on Jewish celebrations. In fact, we didn't have them at all. We'd have Christmas and Easter and that was about it, and then we'd go to Renate's family for Pesach.

'Yes,' Renate agrees 'in my family we celebrated Passover but we didn't say any prayers, we just ate. But Peter's family were Yeccher—very assimilated Germanic types.'

Peter says: 'We would have Christmas because everybody in Vienna had Christmas, and we always had a tree and presents and so on.'

'When we got married,' remembers Renate 'and I told my mother we were going to Peter's home for Christmas, she said, "Christmas? Isn't he Jewish? I thought he was Jewish?"'

'I thought it was very funny not having Christmas,' said Peter. 'I would have felt terribly deprived as a child growing up in Australia without getting Christmas presents.'

Renate replies, 'You should have grown up in St Kilda—nobody got Christmas presents.'

The cooking in Peter's childhood home was Central European rather than Jewish—Wiener Schnitzel, Pariser Schnitzel and Natur Schnitzel as well (this was before he was a vegetarian)—and there were plenty of Viennese cakes.

'We had a Kugelhopf which you called a babka, and there were walnut cakes and chocolate cherry cakes and then another cake my mother makes called Pischinger Torte, which is a wafer and cream cake. But Austrian desserts are nor just cakes, there are also eggy desserts like Salzburger-nockerl Knochel and Kaiserschmarrn.'

'I should show you the cookbook that my mother-in-law gave me when we married,' Renate says to me. 'The balance of recipes is very interesting. It's a book as fat as this, and most of the courses take up this little bit of the book, and the rest of the book is devoted to the desserts!'

peter and renate singer's ethical ponchkes

¼ cup (60ml/2fl oz) vanilla soy milk
2 tablespoons (60g/2oz) sugar
2 sachets dry yeast
pinch of salt
cinnamon to flavour
2½ cups (425g/15oz) plain flour
2 egg yolks (free range only)
1 tablespoon (30g/1oz) margarine
plum jam (povidl)
caster sugar for coating

Mix warm soy milk with sugar and yeast and leave for about 10 minutes till frothy.
Add salt, flour and egg yolks and make into a dough.
Leave to prove in a warm place for 2 hours. Work margarine and cinnamon into pastry and form doughnuts. Insert plum jam with a teaspoon. In enough very hot oil for them to float, fry doughnuts until golden brown, and roll in caster sugar.
The quantity it makes will depend on how big you make them.

Lekah
(celebration cake)

When there is a birthday in our family, I always make this nine-egg sponge cake, divide it into three or four layers, put kirsch and marmalade between them, and fill them with mocha cream, which also covers the cake. It towers in the fridge, and comes to the table on an elevated glass cake platform. There are gasps and cheers when the cake arrives, even though we have it every time.

When there is a need for a quiet, dignified cake to have with a glass of tea, Polish-style, or after a meat meal, when you can't have milk for 4 hours, we have tea with a slice of lemon and sugar, and I make this cake without the trimmings, covering it only with a dusting of caster sugar.

You nearly didn't have this recipe because when I began writing this book, Sara, my younger daughter, asked me not to include it, as she regarded it as a family tradition and a family secret. But later she began to waver. Then she cooperated by finding references for me in her Torah, the one she had been given by the Rabbi on the occasion of her Bat Mitzvah, the coming-of-age ceremony. This recipe is given then, with Sara's blessing.

9 eggs, separated
1½ cups (370g/13oz) sugar
1 teaspoon vanilla essence
1½ cups (255g/9oz) plain flour
juice of 1 lemon

Preheat oven to 180°C (350°F). Beat the whites with sugar until they are stiff.
Beat the yolks with vanilla essence until thick.
Add the yolks to the whites and fold in the flour. Add the lemon juice last,
and bake for about 35 minutes, until golden brown.

Variation: hazelnut cake

Replace 1 cup (170g/6oz) plain flour with 1 cup (140g/5oz) ground hazelnuts (filberts),
and the remaining ½ cup (90g/3oz) plain flour with ½ cup (90g/3oz) self raising flour.

Baked cheesecake

Nothing beats a baked cheesecake. Mama used to look down on the Aussie cheesecakes which used cream cheese, gelatin and passionfruit topping. And rightly so.

Pastry:
255g (9oz) butter
1 cup (255g/9oz) sugar and 2 eggs
1 teaspoon vanilla essence
enough ½ plain and ½ self-raising flour to make a pastry (about 2 cups or 340g/12oz)

Combine the butter and sugar in a blender until creamy, then add beaten eggs and vanilla essence. Mix in enough flour to make a pastry and allow to cool in the refrigerator until the cheese filling is ready.

Filling:
1kg (2lbs 4oz) cottage cheese
1¼ cups (310ml/10fl oz) cream
1 cup (255g/9oz) sugar and 2 eggs
1 teaspoon vanilla essence
juice of 1 lemon
1 cup (200g/7oz) sultanas

Preheat oven to 200°C (400°F). Combine the cheese, cream, sugar, eggs and vanilla essence together and beat until smooth. Add the lemon juice and sultanas last, and fold into the mixture. Divide the pastry into two portions: one of two-thirds and one of one third. Roll the larger portion out to about 1cm thick, then line the bottom and sides of a baking dish with it. Prick the pastry all over with a fork. Pour in the cheese mixture, then roll out the remaining pastry and cut into long strips about 3cm (1 inch) wide. Criss-cross the top of the cheesecake in a lattice pattern with the pastry strips, then coat them with milk applied with a pastry brush. Bake at 200°C (400°F) for about 40 minutes, until the pastry is golden brown and the cheese firm.

Mirka Mora is a Melbourne-based artist who emigrated from Paris after the Second World War. She is known for the beautiful fantasy creatures which she brings to life as dolls and which adorn her paintings and sketches, as well as a wall at the Flinders Street train station, and even a Melbourne tram. She ran the Mirka Cafe in the 1950s, and later, the Tolarno Restaurant, with the late Georges Mora.

Mirka Mora opens the door to her terraced cottage in St Kilda, a real doll's house. We squeeze through the entrance into a corridor stacked with paintings (some framed but most not), with books, toys, and furniture lining both sides of the hall. There is even less room to walk than there was a year ago. She has been busy working.

In her kitchen, there are dolls and crockery and antique lacy tea towels and miniature cooking utensils, like the tiny food processor that she winds up with delight. The disorder evaporates, as the eye sees the neat system she has for putting implements away on upright trays that hang from the sides of the cupboards, the ingredients in place in small cupboards, the stacks of dishes and wooden spoons and trays. It is clean. There is a place for everything. There is just so much of everything and so few places to put it.

Newspapers line the floor, and Mirka shows us how they can be replaced with a swoop of the hands, out the back door. Start again! Instead of a refrigerator she has a coolgardie safe with a black plastic bat sitting on the top. She likes bats, and says that when I am an older lady, I should have bats too, because the little boys in the neighbourhood love them, and will always want to visit.

Mirka squats down on the floor, her eyes level with the wooden butcher's bench that she wheels out into the middle of the floor. It takes up all the available space.

'It's a walnut cake, and it's from my childhood. This is how big I was when my mother and my auntie made the cake, and this is how I saw the pile of walnuts, and the pastry. It was sheer childhood delight, because the cakes were delicious, but I cannot separate the cakes from the two sisters. They made it every Saturday afternoon.'

Mirka is trying to remember just how much of the ingredients to use. She shuts one eye and then the other, as if trying to judge perspective in a painting.

'That's when I'm dangerous, Ramona—that's when I'm a gambler. It goes with my mood. Like the tonality of a painting. Do you want a green or a greener green or a yellow green or a blue green or a reddish green? It's very tricky. But I'm going to weigh this up and have a certain structure.

'In this little kitchen there is not much space, but everything is in its place. You have to be very organised if you are a painter. People never understand this, but unless you are, you don't know what you are doing.

'My aunt and my mother were very close, as they were the only two girls in Paris from a big Parisian family. My mother even found my auntie's husband for her. He was a professor of Esperanto, and quite a scholar. As a child I never liked him very much, he was too powerful and I didn't like him coming close to me. He was brilliant, and when the Germans came to Paris, he went out in the street in his underpants, and he was arrested and put into a mental home. Right through the war. And straight after the war, he rang all his friends at the Sorbonne. They said "Oh, he's alright!" and he came out, and found another wife. My poor auntie had been taken to Auschwitz, while he saved his life. He should have saved my auntie's life, but didn't. But wasn't he brilliant to do that?

'I saw him a little bit after the war. I remember his second wife got pregnant, and my uncle didn't want her to have the child. In those terrible days, in 1946, the poor woman couldn't have an abortion, so she climbed onto the top of the wardrobe. I remember her jumping from there onto the floor three or four times. Of course, it never worked, it was an absurdity.

'The cake period was when I was small, and I would listen to the two ladies talking about how bad their husbands were. I've looked at many recipes for walnut cake, but none was as simple as my mother's. Or as simple as my memory of it!

'You don't crush the walnuts at all, that I remember. That's the beauty of this cake, that they were still whole once they were cooked. See how beautiful it looks! Do you think we should add some rum to the walnuts? My mother would not have put in rum. Let's put some rum in it. And make a wish.

'There seems to be a lot of walnuts here, but it's a childhood memory and, let's face it, the memory is the walnuts! A memory is like a dream, if it's out of order it doesn't matter, but for any good cook, this would be too many walnuts. But because I am the cook, and because I am the cook I am, that's how it will be.

'Anybody more reasonable than us would have used less walnuts. Ramona, you are encouraging me, you are dangerous! You may well laugh, but it will be delicious. When you cook, you have to be a gambler. Even if you miss, you have to have had a great adventure!'

mirka mora's walnut cake

Pastry:
310g (11oz) plain flour
170g (6oz) white sugar
3 eggs
90g (3oz) butter
15g (½oz) vanillin flavouring (Dr Oetker's if you can find it)
walnut oil

Mix the ingredients together in a blender to form a pastry. You can add extra flour if the mixture is too sticky. Roll it out into a rectangular shape on a pastry board until the pastry is 3cm (1 inch) thick.

Walnut Filling:
90g (3oz) butter
90g (3oz) brown sugar
500g (1lb 2oz) walnuts
1 small liqueur glass of rum

Additional:
1 egg yolk
1 tablespoon walnut oil

Preheat oven to 210°C (425°F). Melt the butter and the sugar together in a saucepan until the mixture has the consistency of caramel. When the mixture starts to bubble, add the walnuts, then the rum, and stir over a flame. When thoroughly mixed, heap the walnut mixture in a row down the centre of the pastry, and join the outer edges of the pastry together over the mixture, making a cigar shape.
Brush the top of the cake with a wash made from an egg yolk mixed with a tablespoon of walnut oil.
Lift the cake onto a flat baking sheet which has been basted with walnut oil too, and bake
at 210°C (425°) for 20 minutes. Cool on a wire rack.

sara's apple pie

My mother told us that we came from a pastry family. 'We had flour mills in the family before the war' she said with a look to the middle distance, as if she could just make out a silo at the end of the backyard, 'and Grandmother made cakes for her shop.'

Mother made wonderful apple pies, with the pastry made from scratch and using the apples from our tree. Just before the pie went into the oven, she would make a small hole in the top to let the steam out, and around it she would place five or six petals made from the dough set aside for this purpose. A work of art, I thought.

Once when I was ill and had taken to my bed, my daughter Sara said she would cook, and locked herself away in the kitchen. Good, familiar smells came from the oven over the next few hours as I drifted in and out of sleep.

When I went to the kitchen, there was no-one there, but on the bench was an apple pie, with the petals placed gently on the top, just like Mother made, crafted by her granddaughter, the namesake who never knew her.

Pastry:
255g (9oz) butter
1 cup (255g/9oz) sugar
2 eggs
1 teaspoon vanilla essence
enough ½ plain and ½ self-raising flour (about 2 cups or 340g/12oz) to make a pastry

Combine the butter and sugar in a blender until creamy, then add beaten eggs and vanilla essence. Mix in enough flour to make a pastry and allow to cool in the refrigerator.

Filling:
10 large green apples and juice of 2 lemons
140g (5oz) almond meal
1 cup (200g/7oz) raisins
½ teaspoon cinnamon
1 cup (255g/9oz) sugar
1 teaspoon vanilla essence
vanilla sugar and extra cinnamon

Preheat oven to 180°C (350°F). Peel and grate the apples and add the lemon juice to prevent discolouration. Combine with all the other ingredients.
Drain excess apple juice from the bottom of the bowl.
Roll out half of the pastry for the pie base to about 1cm (½ inch) thick. Place it in a large pie dish and prick the base with a fork. Put the filling in, add more cinnamon, and cover with the rest of the rolled pastry, except for a small ball set aside for the leaves. Pinch the edge of the pie together using thumbs and forefingers of both hands and make a small hole at the top of the pie in the middle.
Fashion 5 or 6 leaves or petals out of the remainder of the pastry, and place around the hole. Brush the pie with milk, and dust with vanilla sugar and cinnamon. Bake at 180°C (350°F) for about an hour, or until the pie is golden brown.

variation: apple strudel

You can use the same apple pie filling above for apple strudel. Use sheets of filo pastry instead of shortcrust pastry. Open the filo leaves out and select one, brushing it all over with melted butter, then place another sheet over it. Do this five more times. Layer the filling along one edge. Roll it up, tucking in the ends to seal the strudel. Brush the top with melted butter and sprinkle with sugar and cinnamon. Bake at 180°C (350°F) for 30 minutes. Serve with cream.

variation: cherry strudel

Replace apples with a jar or two of morello cherries, 1½ cups (200g/7oz) almond meal, ½ cup (110g/4oz) sugar and ½ cup (90g/3oz) sultanas.

breads, biscuits and confectionery

There was always a tin of beautiful biscuits in my mother's pantry, for whenever guests might call. We used to sneak them, one by one, and watch 'Sea Hunt' on television. When the tin was getting dangerously low, we worried that Mum would notice. What if visitors came, would we be ashamed? Mother always had an emergency supply of biscuits, a back-up to the back-up. 'No-one ever starved in my house,' she said.

We had emergency tins of fruit and baked beans, tomatoes, sweet corn and asparagus piled high in the cupboards. And stacks of rice and flour, and beans of all descriptions, in jars. You never know what's just around the corner, so always fill the biscuit tin.

mandelbrot
(almond bread)

Makes about 25 slices

These toasted slices of almond pastry are excellent as an accompaniment to tea or coffee in the afternoon, or after a meal.

2 eggs
110g (4oz) caster sugar
6 tablespoons vegetable oil
1 teaspoon lemon juice
4 drops almond essence
90g (3oz) blanched almonds
280g (10oz) plain flour
2 teaspoons baking powder
pinch of salt

Preheat oven to 180°C (350°F). Beat the eggs and sugar lightly, adding
the oil, lemon juice and almond essence. Combine with the coarsely chopped almonds.
Sift the flour, baking powder and salt into a bowl, add the egg mixture and mix into a dough.
Shape into 2 rolls about 7.5cm (3 inches) wide and put them on a well-greased oven tray,
baking at 180°C (350°F) for 30–40 minutes until very lightly browned.
Let the rolls almost cool, then cut into thin slices about 1cm (½ inch) thick.
Return to the oven until they are golden brown.

Halvah shortbread

Makes about 20

This sounds a rather unlikely combination of Glasgow and Alexandria, but trust me, it's delicious.

170g (6oz) butter, softened
½ cup (110g/4oz) tahini and pinch of salt
1¼ cups (255g/9oz) brown sugar and 2 cups (340g/12oz) plain flour
½ cup (60g/2oz) ground almonds and ½ cup (90g/3oz) walnut halves

Preheat oven to 180°C (350°F). With a food processor or by hand, cream the butter with the tahini.
Add the salt and brown sugar. Blend until smooth. Sprinkle in the flour, blending well.
Mix in the chopped nuts. The dough will be very stiff. Lightly butter a shallow baking pan.
Place the dough in pan and press to evenly cover the bottom and sides to a thickness
of no more than 5mm (¼ inch). Press a few nuts into the surface to decorate.
Bake the shortbread for 15 minutes. Remove it from the oven as soon as the edges
are golden brown. Cut into squares while still warm.

spicy Honey Biscuits

Makes about 40

110g (4oz) butter, softened
½ cup (110g/4oz) brown sugar and ½ cup (125ml/4fl oz) honey
1 egg and 2½ cups (450g/1lb) plain flour
2 teaspoons ground ginger
1 teaspoon baking powder
1 teaspoon ground cinnamon and 1 teaspoon ground nutmeg
½ teaspoon salt and ¼ teaspoon ground cloves

Preheat oven to 180°C (350°F). In a large bowl, cream the butter and sugar and then add the honey and egg beating thoroughly. Combine the flour, ginger, baking powder, cinnamon, nutmeg, salt and cloves and add to honey mixture. Beat on low speed until well blended. Cover dough and refrigerate for 1 hour. Roll out to 5mm (¼ inch) thickness. Cut into shapes and place on a greased pan. Bake at 180°C (350°F) for about 10 minutes.

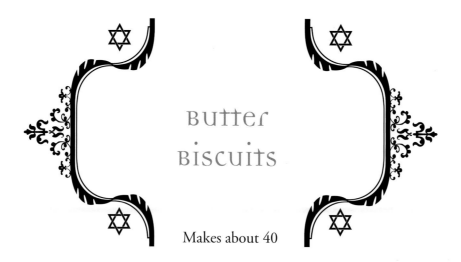

Butter Biscuits

Makes about 40

255g (9oz) butter and 1 cup (255g/9oz) sugar
1 teaspoon vanilla essence
2 eggs
about 2 cups (340g/12oz) plain flour
handful of slivered almonds or mixed peel (optional)

Combine butter and sugar with vanilla essence until creamy, then add the beaten eggs, making sure not to curdle the mixture. Add enough plain flour to form a pastry, and cool in the fridge for 15 minutes. Preheat oven to 200°C (400°F). Roll out on a floured board until 1cm (½ inch) thick, and then cut out biscuit shapes with a glass or biscuit cutter. Decorate with slivered almonds, or mixed peel, and bake in a hot oven for 10–15 minutes, or until golden brown.

To this recipe you can add chocolate or cocoa for chocolate biscuits, almond meal and almond essence for almond biscuits—just make your own fun.

Almond and coconut macaroons

Makes about 50

4 egg whites
2 cups (500g/1lb 2oz) caster sugar
255g (9oz) almond meal
2 tablespoons plain flour
1 teaspoon vanilla essence
½ cup (60g/2oz) shredded coconut

Preheat oven to 180°C (350°F). Beat the egg whites and sugar until stiff peaks form.
Fold in the rest of the ingredients carefully so as not to lose the beaten air.
Place generous teaspoonfuls on a greased baking tray and bake for about one hour.

My mother was a proud woman, she was quiet

and dignified in the street, and she knew just what constituted proper behaviour. She learned at an early age to evaluate a situation without giving her hand away.

When Mother was 14 the war had been raging for 2 years, and she was living in a ghetto with her grandmother, mother and brother. She said that her father had died of pneumonia when she was a baby. He had been only 21 when he swam across an icy river to get back to my grandmother in time for my mother's birth. In fact I later discovered he died after a blow to the head in the fight.

By 1941 my grandmother could see that the ghetto was about to be liquidated and that she must try to save her children. My mother looked like me, with blue eyes and blond hair, Polish rather than Jewish. Grandmother told her that she must leave the family, taking two valuable rings, and travel to Warsaw alone where she would be looked after by a Polish family of her acquaintance. The rings were for buying false papers to see her through her change of identity.

Mother walked the 90km (56 miles) to Warsaw. She found the family, bought the identity papers of a Polish woman of 23, and set about learning to be Catholic in their cellar. She looked after their dog, a great dane called Rolf. The hardest part, she said, was learning to kneel on the stone floor in church. But she dared not move with the discomfort lest others notice that she wasn't used to kneeling in prayer.

When the war ended, she was so used to the role that had saved her life that she had forgotten who she was and how to speak the Yiddish and Hebrew of her childhood. She had even forgotten how to pray. But she re-learned the blessings for the Sabbath candles, the wine and the challah bread once I was born. Because, she said, life goes on. And she told me that having us made her survival mean something.

challah

Makes 2 loaves

Challah is the traditional bread served at the Friday night Sabbath meals. It is made of eggs and yeast, and must be pareve—that is, containing no milk or dairy products, so that it can be served with a meat meal.
Sometimes the challah is made round, for special holidays like the New Year Rosh Hashanah, but for general purposes, the challah is plaited like a thick rope of golden hair.
Challah should be torn from the loaf rather than genteely cut, but if you have to cut it, the slices should be thick doorsteps, to soak up sauces or broth.
The best way to eat challah is to smother it with butter, and then add peanut butter. On the morning after the challah has been baked, if there is any left, you can make French toast by dipping it in eggs and milk and salt, and frying both sides in butter.

¾ cup (190ml/7fl oz) warm water
½ cup (110g/4oz) sugar, plus 2 teaspoons extra
1.3kg (3lb) plain flour, plus 1 tablespoon extra
5 teaspoons active dry yeast
½ cup (125ml/4fl oz) peanut oil, plus 1 tablespoon extra
1 tablespoon salt
2 teaspoons honey
3 large whole eggs
2 large egg yolks
1½ cups (375ml/14floz) hot water
margarine for greasing baking sheet
cornflour for dusting baking sheet

Combine ¾ cup (190ml/7fl oz) warm water with the 2 teaspoons sugar, 1 tablespoon flour and the yeast, stirring until the yeast is dissolved. Let the mixture stand in a warm place for about 10 minutes.
Beat together the oil, salt, remaining ½ cup sugar, honey, whole eggs and the yolks.
Add 1½ cups (375ml/14fl oz) hot water, and beat until the sugar and salt are dissolved.
Add the risen yeast mixture and 2¾ cups of the remaining flour. Beat for 5 minutes.

Add 4 cups of the remaining flour and knead the dough for 10 minutes. Transfer the dough to a large well-oiled bowl, coat the whole surface of the dough with oil by moving the dough around the bowl, and leave it to rise in a warm place, covered with a tea towel for about 2 hours until double in volume. Turn the dough out onto a well-floured board and work in the remaining ½ cup flour. Cover the dough for a further 10 minutes, then halve it, and divide each half into 3 pieces. Roll each piece into a 'snake' 30cm (12 inches) long and 3–5cm (1½–2 inches) wide. Braid 3 pieces together, pinch the ends, and tuck them under the loaf. Do the same with the other 3 pieces. Transfer the loaves to the greased and floured baking sheet.

Glaze:
1 large egg
2 tablespoons sugar
1 tablespoon caraway seeds, if desired

Prepare the glaze by mixing the egg with the sugar, brush the loaves well with it, and sprinkle with the caraway seeds. Preheat oven to 190°C (375°F). Allow the loaves to rise uncovered for another 30 minutes, then bake them for about 40 minutes at 190°C (375°F), or until they are golden brown, and sound hollow when tapped. Makes 2 loaves.

chocolate marzipan biscuits

Makes about 60

6 egg whites
2 cups (500g/1lb 2oz) caster sugar
500g (1lb 2oz) marzipan or almond meal
255g (9oz) dark chocolate, grated

Preheat oven to 180°C (350°F). Beat egg whites with sugar until stiff peaks form.
Fold in marzipan meal and grated chocolate. Using a cool spoon, place generous teaspoonfuls
of the mixture onto a greased oven tray. Bake for 15 minutes at 180°C (350°F).

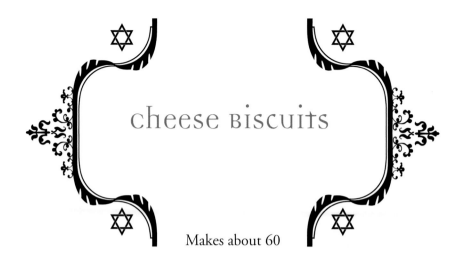

cheese biscuits

Makes about 60

110g (4oz) salted butter
110g (4oz) hard yellow cheese, grated
1 egg yolk
salt
½ teaspoon hot paprika
1 cup (225g/8oz) plain flour

Warm the butter until it begins to melt, then cream it until it is lighter in colour.
Mix in the cheese, egg yolk, salt and paprika and then the flour. Cool the pastry by refrigerating
it for 30 minutes or so. Preheat oven to 200°C (400°F). Knead and roll out to 1cm thickness.
Cut out biscuits using a biscuit shaper, and place on a greased tray. Bake at
the top of the oven for about 10 minutes. Cool and serve.

Toffees (Displaced Persons Camp, Berlin, 1945)

There was to be a fête next morning at school, and our Grade Four teacher said we had to bring things for the stall.

'What things?'

'Oh, you know, fairy cakes, lamingtons, toffees.'

My heart sank. I knew my mother would not know about fairy cakes and lamingtons, so I set my sights on the toffees. These were round and hard and golden, with sprinkles of hundreds and thousands on top. I loved seeing them on the stalls, the paper patty pans decorated with splashes of colour.

'Mama, we have to have something for the stall tomorrow morning. We have to make it now.'

She stopped the treadle machine on which she worked until late into the night, finishing the edges on blouses, sewing buttons on by hand, embroidering the collars.

'So, Rivkele, what do you want me to make for you?'

'Toffees. Do you know what I mean? Toffees. They are hard and golden and you put them in patty pans?'

'Of course I know what toffees are.'

'Really?' My eyes opened wide.

'Really. We used to make them in the DP Camp in Berlin in 1945. We made them out of the condensed milk that the American soldiers gave us. They gave us chewing gum and chocolate, and stockings, too. We had fires out in the cold night air, we huddled around them, and opened a can of condensed milk, and we heated it over the flames and stirred it with a stick, and then it turned into toffee. Simple!'

My eyes narrowed. I became suspicious. I knew that the other mothers in my class did not learn their cooking secrets in DP Camps in Berlin.

'Are you sure they will be the same as the other kids' toffees? They must be the same!'

'Have I ever disappointed you?'

So I watched at her elbow as she opened the can, just like she did in the ruins of Berlin, and she turned on the Kooka stove with the laughing kookaburra on the oven door, and we stood together as the sticky mixture heated and then became thicker, and clung to her wooden spoon.

'Ah, it's ready, see? I told you not to worry.'

We filled each patty pan to the brim, and had 12 toffees sitting on the table. They were not hard, not golden and not decorated with hundreds and thousands. They were creamy white. I thought I would die.

She placed them in a tin, and put it in the fridge. Maybe they would change and be set hard in the morning.

When I woke up I opened the fridge, but they were much the same as the night before. I bravely smiled through breakfast, and thanked her as she put the tin in with my red lunch box. I kissed her at the door and set off for school, feeling like a double agent, a traitor, a bad daughter. I had to get rid of the toffees.

At school all was in readiness for the fête at morning play. A table was set out and the offerings were being placed in their little coloured tins, some of which had their owners' names on them. Lamingtons from a girl called Beth Davies, who was always pressed and clean and decorated her pages with vines and flowers up the side. I wished I could hate her. Cheryl Evans' mother had made beautiful toffees, perfect toffees, toffees made in a nice clean kitchen without the smoke of Berlin and the Americans in the air.

I darted to the table and placed my tin at the back behind some jam rolls and slid away. No one had to know. I disowned my mother's toffees. At play lunch we swarmed into the yard. I didn't dare look at which toffees were moving fast, but I knew which ones would be left. I had a vision of the teacher at the end of play lunch, calling out the names of all the children so they could each come and collect their empty plates, and finding the tin of Berlin DP Camp toffees untouched. Who does this one belong to?

I bought a hard golden toffee from the other end of the table and ran about the yard sucking it. Cheryl Evans almost collided with me, her toffee in her mouth.

'Hey! Look at these, you should get one of these if there are any left. Stickjaws!'

Stickjaws. I had never heard of stickjaws, but my mother had made them. My own mother's creamy toffees had disappeared, into the glad hands of Cheryl and Beth and all the other children.

'My mother made them.' I was firm, but in my heart, I wondered if my mother had ever heard of a fluke.

stickjaw toffees

Makes about 12

1 x 400g (14oz) can condensed milk

Heat condensed milk in a saucepan over medium heat until it begins to change colour to creamy gold. Pour into paper patty pans and cool in fridge.

other people's toffees

Makes about 20

500g (1lb 2oz) white sugar
1 cup (250ml/8fl oz) white vinegar
2 cups (500ml/16fl oz) water

Combine all ingredients and heat until the water boils and the sugar is dissolved.
Continue simmering until mixture turns honey coloured. Pour into paper patty pans and cool.
When set, decorate by sprinkling with 'hundreds and thousands'.

measurements

Throughout this book:
¼ cup = 60ml or 2 fl oz
⅓ cup = 80ml or 3 fl oz
½ cup = 125ml or 4 fl oz
⅔ cup = 160ml or 6 fl oz
¾ cup = 190ml or 7 fl oz
1 cup = 250ml or 8 fl oz

1 teaspoon = 5ml
1 tablespoon = 20ml
1 dessertspoon = 12ml

oven temperatures

125°C = 240°F = Very slow
150°C = 300°F = Slow = Gas Mark 2
180°C = 350°F = Moderate = Gas Mark 4
200°C = 400°F = Moderately hot = Gas Mark 6
220°C = 450°F = Hot = Gas Mark 7
250°C = 500°F = Very hot = Gas Mark 9

index

Published in Australia in 2009 by New Holland Publishers (Australia) Pty Ltd
Sydney • Auckland • London • Cape Town
1/66 Gibbes Street Chatswood NSW 2067 Australia
218 Lake Road Northcote Auckland New Zealand
86 Edgware Road London W2 2EA
80 McKenzie Street Cape Town 8001 South Africa

A record of this book is held at the National Library of Australia

ISBN 9781741108521

Publisher: Fiona Schultz
Publishing Manager: Lliane Clarke
Production Manager: Olga Dementiev
Design: Tania Gomes
Photographer: Robert Reichenfeld
Food Stylist: Carolyn Fienberg, Home Economist: Justine Poole
Printer: SNP/Leefung Printing Co Ltd (China)

Publishers' Acknowledgements

The Publishers wish to thank:
The Great Synagogue of Sydney (particularly Susan Bures),
Mr Joseph Ezekiel of the Sephardi Synagogue at Bondi Junction,
Rabbi Jeffrey Cohen and staff at the Jewish Museum of Sydney,
The Kashrut Authority of NSW,
Barbara Wojciechowski of Soos Bakery
and Mr & Mrs Ron and Frances Lowe
for their kind co-operation with this project.

Accessories provided by Ruby Star Traders, Empire Homewares,
The Bay Tree, Papaya, Freedom Homewares and Shalom Gift Shop.